Summer
READING LIST 2023

J.P.Morgan

"*A fascinating history of the Napa Valley over five decades, Tor weaves a year of grape growing and winemaking into a joyful recollection of those characters who continue to define both past and present of this extraordinary 'patch of dirt.' What shines through is a love and deep understanding of wine and food but also an awareness of how fortunate he has been through his long and engaging adventure with wine.*"

—James Simpson, MW, managing director of Pol Roger Portfolio

"*I found Tor's book on food and wine leading the growth of Napa Valley to the position it holds in the world today to be very enlightening. Tor's ability to produce one of the best Cabernets in Napa is not surprising, if one reads this book. Reflections of a Vintner is a terrific read, and bravo to Tor for what he has done for food and wine in Napa Valley—and for doing it in partnership with his wife, Susan, who was and is more than a full partner.*"

—Sanford I. "Sandy" Weill, chairman emeritus of Citigroup

"*We forget sometimes that the Napa Valley's greatness as a wine region has really only happened over a few recent decades and that many of the protagonists of that story are still at it. Mr. Kenward puts readers in the cellars, vineyards, board rooms, and dining rooms where it all happened. It's a riveting bit of history still being written.*"

—Virginie Boone, Napa/Sonoma editor of *Wine Enthusiast*

Dedicated to Susan—
Never
have you stopped me from chasing windmills and dreams.
You're on most every
page of this book.
Thank you,
always.

TOR KENWARD

REFLECTIONS OF A VINTNER

STORIES AND SEASONAL WISDOM FROM
A LIFETIME IN NAPA VALLEY

FOREWORDS BY **ROBERT M. PARKER JR.**
AND **THOMAS KELLER**

CAMERON + COMPANY
Petaluma, California

CONTENTS

FOREWORD

BY ROBERT M. PARKER JR.

THE FINEST WINES OF CALIFORNIA are as multidimensional, profound, and compelling as any wines made in the world. Moreover, the golden age of winemaking in California that started in the early nineties has continued unabated since. Ironically, when I first went to Napa in the seventies, I was blown away by what appeared to be a viticultural paradise, with consistent sunshine, low humidity, and low rainfall—in short, perfect growing conditions. Ripeness was never an issue, but so many California wines seemed to emerge from a philosophical school that emphasized the manufacturing process, producing excessively acidified blends from different parcels with little respect for individual terroir or microclimates. Furthermore, thanks to overly cautious enologists, wineries were excessively filtering wines to the point where no perceptible aromas, textures, or charateristics were left due to the abusive manipulation. Additionally, crop yields were excessive, and the wines were in large part boring and devoid of character.

This time-honored philosophy of California winemaking, which dominated the post-Prohibition era through the late eighties, changed abruptly. By 1990, the obsession with the vineyard as a manufacturing plant and industrial winemaking in the cellars moved from those monolithic, simplistic, and squeaky-clean wines to majestic, complex, rich elixirs that were stunningly perfumed, extraordinarily textured, and intensely rich and full. Their terroir and microclimates were reflected in the final product, whether they emerged from the valley floor or the eastern or western mountainsides. The frightfully acidic and nearly undrinkable harsh, hollow wines of the seventies and eighties turned into beautifully handcrafted works of art that reflected their terroir, the vintage, and the varietal character. Moreover, they provided immense pleasure.

This dramatic shift started around 1990, and the consumer has been the amazing beneficiary of a less traumatic and less interventional wine philosophy that emphasizes the importance of the vineyard's fruit and preserving its characteristics in the most natural method possible. The old days of processed, stripped, distressingly uninspiring wines are long gone.

This shift was aided and abetted by the financially devastating phylloxera epidemic, which allowed viticulturalists and winery owners the silver lining of replanting their vineyards and addressing rootstocks, along with clonal choices and adjusting to the microclimate and soils of their particular property. More vineyards were planted with tighter spacing, and the trend toward organic and even biodynamic viticulture in many places has resulted in increasingly high-quality grapes and, consequently, better and better wines. As time has passed, the phylloxera epidemic has turned out to be a costly yet ultimately positive influence by forcing producers to largely correct the mistakes made in the forties, fifties, and sixties.

Of course, Tor Kenward has been at the epicenter of these significant changes in California winemaking and viticulture, in his unique position as someone who began in winery hospitality, public relations, and human resources but is now an experienced and long-term insider producing his own wines. He's had a front-row, then center-stage, seat during these dramatic events and this extraordinary success story. On Tor's watch, Napa has become one of the great wine-producing regions of the world. When I started as a wine critic over forty years ago, I never dreamed that wines from my own country, especially California, could rival and even surpass the greatest legendary wines of France, Spain, Italy, or Germany. They have done that and have done it consistently over the last thirty years. Tor's contribution, in both wine production and wisdom, has now brought these stories to life.

FOREWORD

BY THOMAS KELLER

I ARRIVED IN THE NAPA VALLEY IN 1992, determined to share my love of cooking, eventually becoming the chef and proprietor of a restaurant called the French Laundry, in a place that was not yet known for its food.

What it was known for was wine. And in 1992, Tor Kenward was already a skilled Napa vintner, studying every inch of the valley as he worked toward his vision—a dreamer's vision—of what wine could be.

In the years to come, I and others were influential in putting Napa on the culinary map. In the process, we were helped immensely by Tor and his colleagues because they attracted people who came for a sublime experience.

Over his decades-long career, Tor worked for—and learned from—some of Napa's brightest lights, leaving his own mark under their labels. Then, just a few years after I opened my first Bouchon in Yountville, he retired. But Tor being Tor, "retirement" was when he began one of the American winemaking world's great second acts: founding his own label and nurturing grapes from start to finish.

By then he'd been in Napa Valley nearly thirty years. Three decades invested in this land. But that's one of the fundamental aspects of how a true winemaker, how Tor, thinks. They see something in the land and nurture it for years, for decades, until under their guidance it reveals a treasure.

Terroir. Legacy. Dedication. These are Tor's ties to Napa and to the craft of making inimitable wine.

This book, which describes so much of what made Tor the Napa Valley icon he is, is a welcome addition to the winemaking canon.

Thankfully, it's not the last word. Tor's wealth of experiences and knowledge could never be contained in one text. He continues to nurture and develop the soil, the culture, and the story of Napa Valley.

*Laura Cunningham and Thomas Keller
in the French Laundry kitchen, 1992*

INTRODUCTION

I HAVE READ A LOT OF WINE BOOKS in the last fifty years. Some changed my life forever, some were wasted on me, and for some, a tooth extraction would be more welcome—I didn't finish those in the last category, nor are they in my library, but the pretty ones do end up in the guest bathrooms. Hugh Johnson's first paperback edition of *The World Atlas of Wine*, with its detailed maps of vineyards and wineries, rode in my lap in the eighties and nineties through most of the wine-growing regions of France, Italy, Spain, Portugal, and Germany. Before GPS, this dog-eared book got me to all my appointments on time.

I hosted Hugh for a book-signing party and dinner decades later—he signed my beaten-up book, and I bought the updated edition. We had some good laughs and drank several glasses of wine while reminiscing. Many of the books in my library are signed, and I have joyfully shared a table and wine with most of the authors.

I hosted M. F. K. Fisher in the eighties for lunch, wine, and storytelling, but I was too embarrassed to ask her to sign her books. I was awed by her gift of storytelling. I still am. One signed favorite, *Adventures on the Wine Route*, by Kermit Lynch, is full of stories about the people behind the wines, giving them flesh and color in our minds. That is the direction I have taken here.

I have lectured and taught all things wine for four decades. I've been on *60 Minutes*, CNN, and *The Today Show*, and in and out of most major airports, as an ambassador of wine. Thankfully, I learned that talking to large groups about winemaking and the complex science and numbers associated with making wines did not inspire. My audience preferred to talk over me or daydream, or both. I didn't take it personally because I had seen other vintners fall into this death trap.

Wine-speak can be numbing to those who are not as obsessed as those of us who make wine our life's purpose. When I shared stories about the people I had met through wine, mentors like Julia Child, Robert Mondavi, and André Tchelistcheff, the room fell silent. I had their attention. I became more of a storyteller as I traveled outside my Napa Valley, and more of a winemaker inside my Napa Valley.

Fast-forward to 2020. Like most of us, I was given time to sort through my past as the present and future stood still. I began to write the stories—stories about people who had changed or shaped my life as a vintner—and posted them on our TOR Wines website. The response was positive and instant, and oddly addictive. I wanted to get it all written down. The drug was taken away from me when my agent, Leslie Stoker, told me I couldn't post any more of these stories. They needed to go into a book. And here we are.

Writing this book reminded me how much the wine business, deep in its heart of hearts, is all about relationships. It's about partnerships based on respect and trust, and how they form and strengthen over time. My decades living the life of a prominent vintner in Napa Valley has proved this point without interruption. Money will buy you a lot of things, even a winery, but it doesn't buy your way into the best vineyards in the valley. Respect and friendships do. I love the wine business for this.

When I arrived in Napa Valley in the mid-seventies, there were no destination restaurants or hotels—no destination anything. The mantra with the growers and tasting rooms managers was, "Do not let the sun set on the tourists." There were less than fifty wineries. Today, we have destination everything—three-star Michelin restaurants, four-star hotels, and theme park wineries. Most everyone I know who works in the wine industry wants the sun to rise on the tourists. Bring them on! Oh, yes, and we now have over eleven hundred wine brands that call Napa Valley home.

How did all that happen in fifty years? This is the story. I was there, on the leading edge of a huge wave that changed the contours of the wine industry and a little place on Earth called Napa Valley. I tell my journey as a vintner through the people who led the charge and made history.

I can honestly say I have worn all the hats and done all the jobs that a vintner can do. I worked hard from the bottom up and—with the rose-colored glasses of hindsight—had a ball. All the rich people who made a small fortune in the wine business by investing their large fortune—where's the fun in that? Delegating all the hard jobs to others lessens the adventure and dumbs down the joys. Delegating? I have been miserable at this. No ghostwriter for this guy. No filter. Let this mad old man get up on the table and make a fool of himself. Hopefully, he has a few moves left.

I begin this dance with a step into a winemaker's life for a calendar year. January takes the lead with tasks a winemaker confronts and thinks about during the month. It's not all romance. Winemaking is hard work. Once the tasks are established, I launch into the Napa Valley stories—my life as a vintner the last nearly fifty years in the valley. The dance expands into a life surrounded by colorful people, big dreamers, mighty madmen, and dastardly villains—they're all in the mix. In a strange way, this is a coming-of-age story. I have never grown up, so this is not my pathway to adulthood. It is Napa Valley's coming-of-age story.

Oh, and did I say this already? It is all about relationships.

Tor and Andy Beckstoffer at the French Laundry to promote an auction lot supporting local charity. The lot was appropriately titled, "A Night at the French Laundry with Two Wild and Crazy Guys." We raised good money and tried to live up to the hype.

You Americans have the loveliest wines in the world, you know, but you don't realize it. You call them domestic, and that's enough to start trouble anywhere.

—H. G. WELLS
BRITISH WRITER AND SOCIAL REFORMER, 1866–1946

JANUARY

I'VE ALWAYS FELT THAT JANUARY is a fresh start. I can look back at two vintages in the barrel, make good assessments on the oldest wines, rough ones on the new wines. A hands-on winemaker walks the rows of the new wines in barrels and listens. Wine whisperer. What we listen for is the sound of fermentations, primary and secondary. Primary converts sugars to wine, and the carbon dioxide given off is audible. Secondary converts malic acids to lactic acids and is also audible to the trained ear. Both are natural and don't need encouragement in nature most of the time. But sometimes, nature is finicky and needs a little traffic direction to get home. The winemaker listens to, or at the very least pays attention to, each barrel to make sure the wine finds its way home. Blind faith.

The vines are dormant; it is cold outside and often wet. We light fires inside our homes and work on projects pushed into a new year. Clean up and mend vineyard and garden infrastructures on dry days. I like to think anything is possible for the new year, a new vintage. Time to flex those optimism muscles.

Optimism is important in winemaking; the glass better be half full, not half empty, to get through a difficult harvest, and I've had many. I believe this is true when we are young, making choices on the roads or pathways that shape our lives, our families, and generations to come. A simple encounter can send us spinning in new directions and into the unknown without warning or reason. In this chapter, I explore a few of these encounters. Like a pinball guided by chance encounters, I ended up in a foreign land: Napa Valley. The first leg of this vintner's odyssey. A glass half full helped the journey.

SALT OF THE EARTH

I'm a Curious George type. I encourage everyone in my tastings to openly express ideas, criticism, and applause if appropriate. One day, I had a very famous golfer volunteer to show me he could shimmy on his back across the floor with great agility. People have been known to climb onto tabletops and break out into sudden bursts of singing during our wine tastings. One night, I was lifted onto a chandelier to test its footings. No one has ever been hurt. Wine has been spilled, but the band plays on.

We've made a lot of friends over my half century of sharing our wine, breaking bread. Many contact me regularly with thanks and celebratory notes. No complaints that I can remember. But maybe that is a subjective choice. It is a good job making the best wine you can from Napa Valley grapes and sharing it with others. It's served me well—it's too late to change direction now, and I have no interest. Before winemaking, I had a jazz club with friends for a few years. I even served as a bodyguard for Elvis and Aretha Franklin. One-night gigs. Didn't last long. Stuck with winemaking, being a vintner. I've made some good choices in my life. We won't discuss too many of the bad ones here, but there are some.

During one tasting not long ago, someone in the group commented how all the young Cabernets that day were beginning to taste too tannic and bitter. I think we have very polished, pixelated tannins in our young wines. However, if you don't stay in training as my winemaker and I do, I get it. The thirtieth young Cabernet Sauvignon on the third day of your visit to Napa Valley might make your tongue feel like it's been in a bar fight. Purple haze. Professional winemakers and wine critics stay in training, but I'm sympathetic to the untrained boxer new to the gym.

I went to the kitchen and grabbed the wooden jar that holds a special salt my wife and I like to use and brought it to the table. I then invited anyone who wanted to participate in my little trick to take a taste of a young Cabernet. Everyone did. Then I asked them to put a little salt on their hand and lick it, then taste the same wine again. They all did. Everyone's face lit up.

WOW, THIS WINE HAS REALLY OPENED UP

I've heard this statement in the evening during a long meal with wine and friends. A good dinner party is a way of decanting some people, allowing them a little air to open up and enjoy themselves with friends. Some are amusing to others, some only to themselves. In vino veritas.

Their comments described how the wine was immediately "rounder," "smoother," "less tannic." And the wine was. Salt has the amazing ability to soften the tannins in a young wine. Think about all those steak houses and which two common ingredients are added to the steak before it gets to your plate: salt and butter. Both can make a youthful Cabernet a bit less rambunctious or simply delicious. It is no accident that steakhouses in all fifty states sell a lot of Cabernet Sauvignon. Salt, fat, and red wine "go together like a horse and carriage"—all together now.

"Wow, this wine has really opened up tonight." How often have you heard that phrase during a wine-oriented dinner party? I have on more occasions than I can count—and I'm good at math. Two things have taken place: There is salt, fat, and/or butter on the table, and the wine has changed. The third possibility is that after a few glasses of wine, the participant has opened far more than the wine being consumed. Another dancer on the tabletop.

Julia Child, who needs no introduction, and Madeleine Kamman, who might but was a very brilliant chef, teacher, and writer; both taught me the salt trick. Both inspired many young chefs, whether professional or amateur, to love cooking and sharing the table. I'm very fortunate to have known them as friends.

Madeleine would put salt, lemon juice, and sugar on the table, and we would play around with wines to see how they worked together. I invite you to try this if you love wine and are interested in the complex cause and effect of simple ingredients. It is how these ingredients are combined that creates great wine-and-food pairings.

Fish with red wine. Steak with a Chardonnay. Roquefort or blue cheese with a sweet wine like Sauternes. They all work and can be swimmingly brilliant wine and food partners. Please don't get locked into the rules you've heard all your life. Play a little, experiment, and you will find some conventional wine-and-food pairings are fanciful fairy tales. Get off the beaten path, try that road less traveled, get some new scenery into the picture. A little dash of salt, lemon, or soy sauce (umami) can take you places you thought you'd never go.

Instead of cheeses and red wine, try simple, well-made (homemade if possible) salted potato chips. Really. Most cheese plates served with red wine would go better with simple, unoaked white wines. A harder cheese like Parmigiano-Reggiano can sing choruses with some red wines. It's used in several tasting rooms in Napa Valley, paired with Cabernets that cost over $500 a bottle. Candidly, I think a bowl of fresh salted potato chips make the wines almost as good a partner, but they are not as sexy as a gorgeous chunk of Parmesan or a thin slice of jamón ibérico. Salt and fat—and no, you don't need the cow's milk; a fresh olive oil can work miracles.

Last trick. Taste a young red wine after our salt experiment. Now, lick a little sugar off your hand and try that red wine again. The fruit has somehow left the station, and the bitterness of the red wine is parked in its place. Avoid a lot of sugar in any dish with a dry red or white wine if you want to taste the grape. A simple down-and-out rule.

Sergeant A. Tor Kenward—Dong Tam, Vietnam, 1969

In 1969, I was in Vietnam, serving the last seven months of my tour in evacuation hospitals, mostly in the southern Delta. The world I lived in was a lot like *M*A*S*H*. It was a crazy, heartbreaking rite of passage. In retrospect, I was young, and with immaturity came some resilience and a little madness with some of the risks I took. One night, I broke the rules and left the evacuation hospital to visit a Vietnamese civilian who worked at our PX store near the hospital. (A PX, or post exchange, is similar to a current-day Target.) His invitation promised I would have one of the most amazing meals of my life if I met him at a location near a fishing village. My only ticket was a bottle of Johnnie Walker Black, which I bought from the PX.

I was intrigued and stupid for putting myself in a place where I had no protection. It was off-limits for good reason. I did not come armed, and I was dressed in civilian clothes. That was the deal. It could have been a deadly setup, but I had enjoyed my conversations with this well-educated older Vietnamese gentleman who'd invited me. I trusted him after many encounters.

Near sunset, I paid a boy-son to drive me on his motorcycle to the fishing village. My civilian friend greeted me and then guided us to a table on one of the boats, where we watched other boats pull into shore just as the sun set. The view and the peacefulness were unforgettable, just like the meal we shared while drinking his bottle of watered-down Johnnie Walker Black.

Over the next hour, my Vietnamese civilian would walk to every small fishing boat as it was pulled onshore and inspect the catch. Most of the catch was shellfish, most of it still alive. He was very particular about his selections and enlisted help preparing the catch for our dinner. I was the honored guest.

The shellfish and shrimp were so fresh and sweet, unlike anything I had experienced in my young life. I loved fresh fish and still do. My father didn't, so it was a luxury reserved for my birthdays growing up. My meal that night set a bar that has been matched in Michelin-starred dining rooms, but it hasn't been surpassed. I think of that meal now when people talk about the most unforgettable meals of their lives.

My Vietnamese host had one sauce other than the watered-down Black that he served with the prepared fish. It was simply lemon juice and salt stirred together. We dipped the sweet fish and ate to our hearts' content. It was dark when I left. I made it home safely, in some ways a different man.

Salt follows us wherever we go. It is always there, opening up worlds for us. Salt has been the foundation of some cultures, where it has been prized more than gold. It's there in times of war and peace. Like wine, it can bring people together. It was a wise man who proclaimed we are the salt of the earth.

THE ROAD TO NAPA

My first business trip to Napa Valley, in 1975, was as a wine scout for two retail wine-and-liquor stores, and the journey was not linear. Like many others in their early twenties, I had spent a year in Vietnam and returned whole but scattered. I wanted to distance myself from my year in Vietnam. I had worked the hospitals from Saigon into the Delta and saw a lifetime of carnage. On my return, I tried consciously to discover ways to celebrate life, detach from war and its memories.

Dad was a writer—actually made a decent living at it for a few years. His first play, *Cry Havoc*, was the most celebrated work of his long writing career, and the only one that was truly successful. It was big in every way in 1944. It went from a Los Angeles playhouse to Broadway and then was made into a film starring Ann Sothern, Joan Blondell, and Margaret Sullavan. Showcasing an all-woman cast and revolving around nurses in the Philippines during World War II, it entertained and struck a national nerve. After the fame faded and future scripts were optioned, bought, but never produced, he worked as a script doctor and kept writing to the age of ninety-four. But he never sold or produced another play or movie. Such is the biz.

Mom was a painter, a very good one with real talent. She studied and loved the cubists. She sold a few paintings, not as many as she should have, but I am prejudiced. She was beautiful and quiet—a muse for many of us, and it was not until recently that we learned she was an accomplished actress in the thirties on and off Broadway. Such was our mom: quietly inspirational, guiding, and self-effacing. Sadly, she succumbed to Alzheimer's late at age ninety-two, and it broke all of our hearts. So much about her early life was revealed after her death. Both parents were of a generation that did not talk loudly about themselves. It was bad manners and exhibited shallow character.

As a couple, Mom and Dad loved to cook (Dad was the serious cook), entertain, and share their lives with other bohemians. We had actors like Jimmy Cagney put us up when we lost a home to fire and flood in Beverly Glen. (He also wrote me letters while I was in Vietnam.) We had musicians—Dad played reed instruments with a regular recorder group and helped with the scripts for a few Elvis movies. (He thought Elvis was a gentleman but didn't like the music.) Painters involved in the early California watercolor movement, such as Phil Paradise, came to visit Mom. Writers, poets, dreamers, all forms of creative people wandered in and out of the house throughout my youth.

The antithesis of social climbers, Mom and Dad let my brother, two sisters, and me fend for ourselves once we were adults. They did little to shape our lives, for they had already done that. We were bohemians, too, and still are. They named us after characters in the plays they loved: Tor, Rory, Tandy, and Kim. Thank God none of us were called Moonbeam.

I dabbled in the music business in the early seventies, forming a jazz club with a few friends in Santa Barbara. We branched out and booked artists and comedians: Tom Waits, Chuck Berry, Steve Martin, Lily Tomlin, Return to Forever. We started a wine and food group, and I launched my trips to Napa and Sonoma, looking for wines to share with my friends. Then, one day in 1977, after a successful sold-out concert for Keith Jarrett, I took the money and ran to Napa Valley to apply for work and residence.

My first job in Napa Valley lasted twenty-six years. Luck was my lady.

LADY LUCK

Luck be a lady tonight. In his day, Sinatra found the best lyricists and surrounded himself with talent, and his recordings still slip in and out of our consciousness, most of us of a certain age when circumstances trigger them. "Luck Be a Lady" triggered memories that led me to reflect on my life as a vintner in Napa Valley the past fifty years.

It was luck that I traveled to Napa Valley and fell in love in the mid-seventies. It was strong women and men who led the way to so many adventures in wine, food, and self-discovery. My wife, who I met at the Napa Valley Wine Auction; my friend and escort, Julia Child; Madeleine Kamman, Lidia Bastianich, Belle Rhodes, and so many other talented and strong women. Robert Mondavi, a mentor on many levels and a Greek tragedy on others. They are part of this narrative, a big part of my life as a winemaker and vintner in Napa Valley.

In the seventies, Napa Valley was a narrow, one-stoplight valley with few restaurants, no themed tasting rooms, not much of anything to attract a tourist other than its wines and its people. *Sunset* magazine listed eighteen

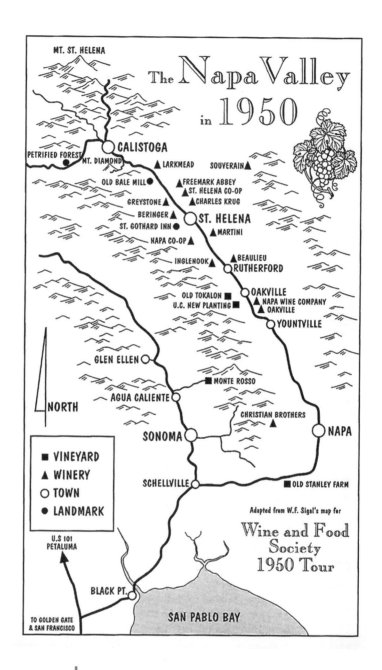

BRIEF NAPA HISTORY—1890: approximately 100 wineries; 1966: 16 wineries; 1995: approximately 200 wineries; 2021: approximately 800 wineries

wineries on its 1968 map. Iconic grape grower Andy Beckstoffer recalls the mantra of the Napa Valley growers and the wineries in the sixties: "We would get together, and the collective voice was, *'Don't let the sun set on the tourists.'* They were not wanted. It was our valley, and they could visit, then leave before sunset." But change was in the air.

Looking back for some perspective, in late 1887, there were over one hundred wineries and 16,661 bearing acres of wine grapes in Napa Valley. The wine business was big business, and the reputation of its wines were sending waves around the world. Gold medals from great world fairs adorned the labels of some Napa Valley wines bragging about their international acclaim.

Between the late 1800s and my first drive through Napa Valley in 1970, however, the valley had suffered internal and external devastation. By the late 1890s, phylloxera (voracious root louse) had brought the wine industries in France and California to its knees. Both continents would have to replant and rebuild their industries.

In most of Western Europe, wine was part of a meal, the rich fabric of each country's culture. In the United States, we had a more puritanical view of wine, which was unwelcome in some religious communities. Wine was not part of our culture. In 1970, the average American consumed 1.3 gallons of wine a year. In France, the average was closer to 30 gallons. The result made the planting and selling of prunes more profitable than wine for most of the early 1900s in Napa Valley, while châteaux in Bordeaux built empires. In 1929, there were more acres of fruit trees (mostly for prunes) than vines in Napa County. Two world wars also shaped our attitude to wine, as did the unenlightened social experiment we called Prohibition. At the end of World War II, brandy, not fine wine, was big business. By 1966, there were sixteen wineries left in Napa County and 11,738 acres of wine grapes, almost half of what there had been in 1890.

By the late sixties, the times were a-changin'. The Vietnam War was in the headlines, and the backlash and protests wove their way deeply into the fabric of our music and media. A wave of new dreamers found their way to the valley to settle and build new wineries. The hope and revolution that was part of the national consciousness was finding its way to sleepy Napa Valley.

I returned from Vietnam in 1969. The GI Bill helped with college and allowed me to dabble in the music industry on the side. Four music fanatics, myself included, who hung out at the local vinyl shops founded a jazz club looking out at the ocean in Santa Barbara. I invested every dollar saved from the Vietnam year (combat pay with nothing to spend it on), and we hosted many of the greats traveling from the Lighthouse in LA to San

Francisco. In this period, I was introduced to the greatest wines in the world by Don Guillette, who ran an idiosyncratic wine shop in the back of a gas station in the poorest part of town. The Grand Crus, First Growths, Grande Champagne, and newbie Napa Valley producers were all open game, as long as I cooked and showed interest. I like to cook and upped my game to match the wines.

In 1976, young rebel winemakers from Napa bested the best from Bordeaux and Burgundy, and Don encouraged me again, as he had in '74 and '75, to go to Napa to hunt down the best of the best. I did, and my life took a radical shift.

I still have the small white paperback notebook where I kept all the acts we booked at our jazz club, surrounding music theaters, and halls. A double billing with Bonnie Raitt and Tom Waits cost us $4,000 to put on. In the same notebook, I kept a list of all the wines I bought on those first trips to the Napa and Sonoma wine regions. I noted two bottles of the 1973 Stag's Leap Wine Cellars Cabernet Sauvignon, purchased from Warren Winiarski for less than twenty dollars. After I tasted and bought the wine, it placed

*Tor under the Golden Gate in the '70s
on a day trip to the Napa Valley*

No thing more excellent nor more valuable than wine was ever granted mankind by God.

—PLATO
GREEK PHILOSOPHER, C. 427–347 BCE

first in the 1976 Paris Wine Tasting. The wine is now showcased in the Smithsonian for its cultural significance. The price, if you can find a bottle today, is $2,300, according to WineBid.com.

Tastings were free in the 1970s, and when I tasted Warren's infamous gem of young Napa vines, I had one of those wine-life epiphanies. It was an underdog and would best Bordeaux's best. It was ethereal—it was the future of Napa Valley and Tor Kenward all bottled up. Then, one day, Joe Heitz tested me on the 1968 Martha's Vineyard Cabernet Sauvignon. I've convinced myself I still can taste that wine, so distinctive, rich, powerful, yet light on its feet, and that forever finish that kept going and going long after I left his small tasting room on Highway 29. Joe refused to sell me a bottle that day. His excuse: "I can get more money for it next year." He was right, but I still carry the scar and memory of walking out empty-handed. Next year, he sold it for over twenty dollars a bottle, and I didn't think I could afford it. No Cabernet Sauvignon from Napa Valley had sold for more than twenty dollars until then. How dare Joe? Again, I have made some bad decisions in my life, including not buying more 1968 Martha's when I first had the chance. I've bought and drank several since for upward of $200. Only one bottle left in the cellar. When I finish this book, I'm drinking it with those who helped.

Much later, Joe's daughter sold me a case of the 1974 Martha's at a very good price. I was an insider then—a working vintner. In 1977, the siren was calling me: "Make wine, not music."

When I listened to that siren, I reflected on New Year's Eve 1972. My friend and my jazz club partner, Steve Cloud, put on Chuck Berry at the Arlington Theatre in Santa Barbara. Chuck was clear he wanted people to come onto the stage and dance if they wanted. The fire marshal was adamant that would not happen, or we would be shut down and lose our license if they did come onstage. Steve explained this calmly to Chuck. The concert started at 11:30 P.M., and Chuck was not happy. At midnight, Chuck invited the audience to the stage. Johnny B. (not so) Goode. I watched in awe as Steve tried to gently push back the crowd. I watched in slow motion as Chuck ripped his amp cord and left town. Everyone in the audience wanted their money back. The music business in Southern California in the seventies had great highs and lows, literally and figuratively, and lots of attitude.

Meanwhile, further north, the sirens continued to call. In 1976, Steve Jobs and Apple sold their first computer not far from Napa Valley. The wild and unpredictable Oakland Raiders won the Super Bowl. Steve and I sold out a Keith Jarrett concert at Arlington (the same theater Chuck Berry had abandoned), and I had a little cash in my pocket. *Rumours* by Fleetwood Mac played everywhere because we listened to the radio back then. It snowed in Miami, and I traveled again to Napa Valley to buy more wine. I stopped in San Francisco that year to run the Bay to Breakers. Wanting to spend what little money I had on wine, I camped at the Bothe–Napa Valley State Park campground the next day and woke up the following morning very clear about my future.

I was moving to Napa Valley to be a winemaker. I'd take any job they would give me, but I would make wine and live in Napa Valley. I knocked on doors and asked around. No winemaking jobs, but tour guide, maybe. My girlfriend loved the romantic, castle-like Beringer Rhine House, so I left my makeshift résumé there. They called. I took the job. Lasted a long time. In three years, I was vice president (in charge of all the fun) at Beringer Vineyards. I took winemaking courses at the University of California, Davis, and earned an associate degree in viticulture. I was all in. We had a core group of dreamers at Beringer in those formative years: the executive committee, which stayed intact most of my twenty-five years. We worked well together and were prepared to make noise—build wineries, buy wineries, make excellent wine at all price points.

I retired in 2001 to start my own winery. Beringer threw me a large "retirement" party, and I was properly roasted by family, friends, other vintners from all over the valley, and coworkers. I insisted I was not retiring, just "changing lanes." I finally had enough money to make my original

THE DIE IS CAST

Beware of wines that don't push your buttons in their youth. A good wine needs to be flirtatious, not too mysterious. If something truly bothers you in a young wine—the tannins, the acidity, the oak, the alcohol, the basic flavors—it will continue to bother you as the wine ages. In fact, it often becomes more pronounced with age. Tannin can outlive the fruit. Trust me.

dream come true. It had taken twenty-five years, but I had a wine education you could not buy. I had lessons from many of wine's greatest mentors—and, equally important, I had listened. I had worked from the bottom up and worn all the hats available off a vintner's hat rack.

For twenty-five years I had fanatically immersed myself in Napa Valley—its wines, its complex but fascinating terroir—and I knew the small pieces of vineyard land, the crown jewels of the valley, that I wanted to make wine from. I knew the growers and families who owned them. I had their respect. Some were vineyards that only an insider could have access to, and I was an insider, accepted by the second- and third-generation Napa-ites as a local. I was ready, and I did have a fire in my belly to swing for the fences—make the very best wines I possibly could, forget the costs, climb the ladder, or go up in flames. My family was behind me. The stage was set, the timing perfect.

Twenty years later, I celebrated this decision with dozens of milestones. I was working with many of the most respected vineyards in Napa Valley. My family still supported me, and I supported them. My winemaker still loves to come to work after twenty years of making my wines. The wine critics this anniversary year awarded us seven 100-point scores, four 99-point scores, and ten 98-point scores on our wines from the 2018 vintage. My friend, golfer Phil Mickelson, won the PGA Championship and became the oldest golfer in history to win a major. He drank my wine out of the Wanamaker Trophy and posted the video and a shout-out on his website. I wrote a book about my journey. I became a grandfather. When the Paris Tasting was restaged in Napa Valley in 2021, my wine was #1, replacing Warren's Stag's Leap Cabernet Sauvignon on the podium

Ladies and gentlemen, you just can't make this stuff up. Some may not believe you. Welcome to the twelve months of a winemaker's year, which turned into a journey of a lifetime. It's all true. I was there.

Wine makes daily living easier, less hurried, with fewer tensions and more tolerance.

—**BENJAMIN FRANKLIN**
AMERICAN AUTHOR, SCIENTIST, AND DIPLOMAT; 1706–1790

FEBRUARY

FEBRUARY OFTEN BRINGS FALSE SPRING to Napa Valley. By this, I mean the daffodils bloom, and we often see temperatures hover in the seventies for a few days. The days are short. False springs can lure you into thinking spring is tomorrow. Somehow, true spring always comes when the days lengthen, and the sun is more direct on the vines. Meanwhile, fields of mustard begin to bloom, and tourists pull to the side of the road for Instagram photos. Man, I love those cloudless blue skies and fields of yellow mustard between the vineyards. You never tire of that image, no matter how many years you live here.

The vines do not like a false spring. The warm temperature could trigger them into thinking it is spring and bring new bud growth. A hard frost might destroy the new growth and severely damage a vintage. In some extreme growing regions, it can kill vines. I have not seen the latter in Napa Valley. With February comes prudence and caution. Pruning season begins in earnest. The old wood is removed, and the right amount of new wood and buds is determined and left on the vines. Out with the old; in with the new.

I try to keep my winemaker's vision clear in February and avoid sucker punches. I get my first honest tastes of the previous vintage. This is when we rack the young wines off the lees as they finish their secondary malolactic fermentation. To be sure, we run lab samples on all the wines to confirm they have gone through malolactic fermentation. Some vintages surprise us when using the natural yeasts from the vineyards for our fermentations; some get stuck or just take forever to finish. You need to be careful, run the numbers, pay attention. Taste, listen, smell, use all the senses. Pray.

As winemakers, we have one classroom a year to learn as much as we can. One. The more harvests we work, and the more vintage wines we make, the more most of us realize we will never know it all. The curve goes against us and reminds us each year how much we don't know, not how much we know. Counterintuitive, but real.

In this chapter, I profile two of the most revered and influential winemakers in Napa Valley history: André Tchelistcheff and Robert Mondavi. André, like Harvey Penick, one of golf's great teachers, taught me simple but profound lessons that shaped my winemaker's head. Like Harvey, he was a great mentor to many. Bob Mondavi taught me the value of shaping a vision and staying true to it against adversity.

LUNCH WITH THE MASTERS OF NAPA VALLEY

Soon after I made Napa Valley my home, Myron Nightingale, Beringer's winemaker from 1971 to 1980, invited me to a lunch that I will never forget. Myron was mischievous, devious, and brilliant. He had been making wine in California for three decades and had the full respect of his peers. We were beginning to work together on the shape and marketing of new wine programs for Beringer, the Private Reserve Cabernet program being central in the early days.

I had no place at that lunch other than being an observer. Myron did, as did Robert Mondavi, Louis Martini, André Tchelistcheff, and a few other winemakers and winery proprietors. It was the locals shooting the breeze, all subjects open to discussion. Casual, no one taking notes. The location was the Grapevine Inn, now home to Brix restaurant. Please understand that at the time, there were very few restaurants to have a warm lunch—or dinner, for that matter. Nada. The Grapevine Inn was as good as you could do: no AC, just the basic sandwiches, salads, and steak. And the locals.

Memory has it as 1978, and the room held over a century of winemaking knowledge that memorable day. I kept my mouth shut for the most part, unless spoken to. I listened, and I learned. Some of what I heard shaped my thinking about wine and winemaking over the next four decades.

André Tchelistcheff

I honestly don't remember who asked the big question that resulted in a friendly argument: "What makes a wine age and become better over time?"

When André gave his opinion, I was fascinated and a bit puzzled with his answer, but over time came clarity and vindication.

André was a Russian-born, French-trained enologist. He was brought to Napa Valley by Georges de Latour in 1938 and, while at Beaulieu Vineyard, made many of the valley's greatest twentieth-century wines. Though short in stature, he was a huge, monolithic influence on Napa Valley's coming of age. Many have said he was as important as Robert Mondavi, but he had a completely different personality. He was a quiet leader.

I met André in 1977. His door was always open to anyone who had a question or just wanted to pick his brain. In some way, he influenced every great winemaker in California. Grgich, Winiarski, Mondavi—just about every influential Napa Valley winemaker in the twentieth century was mentored by André. His titles are the Dean of American Winemaking, the Maestro, and the Winemaker's Winemaker. None of us were untouched by his wines or his mentoring.

I might be off on who exactly took which side of the argument, but I do remember the various opinions that made sense when you have a table loaded with experienced winemakers and (maybe as important) serious wine drinkers.

"It's the tannins in the red wines."

"It's the acid, especially in the white wines."

"No, it is a good pH—must be under 4, mid-3s much better."

"It's a wine grown in the right locations that makes all these things possible. Terroir!"

"Not really, gentlemen. It is the balance of all these things that ultimately makes a wine great and gives it longevity." This was Robert Mondavi's argument. "A wine needs to be in balance."

André's contribution to the conversation is the part I distinctly remember. It has stayed with me, and I feel very strongly that he hit a key point that winemakers often overlook. He was also the last one to throw his cards down

WHAT MAKES A GREAT WINE?

Great grapes grown in an extraordinary plot of dirt. It also needs people who have the experience to stay out of the way, yet know when the time is right to interrupt the dance or change the music. Greatness rides the coattails of perception. In the end, it is personal. I wish more people embraced this.

on the table and speak. With André, I always felt there was a hint of theater in his manner that complemented the warm twinkle in his eyes. His thick Russian accent was gentle and modulated, and he never seemed in a rush, unlike Mondavi, who was always quick with his speech and opinions, and most often right.

"No, it is the flesh—it is the flesh in the great wines I have made that seems to give them grace with age," André said. "It is the flesh."

Then he rambled off some of his favorite vintages, the ones that were legendary wines: 1947, 1958, 1968. "They all had flesh in their youth, flesh with age, longevity," André contended.

I must admit I was a bit confused at the time, but with age, "flesh" became crystal clear. The great wines I have tasted or have made had "flesh." They had a texture, a certain ripeness, but it was in proportion to the wine, never a hint of over-ripeness. It was not overblown but compelling in its youth and with age. It had layers of flavors; it convinced you to have another sip and, with age, another glass. Those are the great wines. Those are the wines that age.

I am blessed to have experienced many of the legendary wines in my life. Two classic examples of André's point are the 1947 Cheval Blanc and the 1959 Domaine de la Romanée-Conti and La Tâche (DRC). I was able to buy these while in the wine trade when they were affordable and accessible as a wine professional and exporter. I followed these wines over the years with great joy. There was bottle variation (another story), but all the best bottles had "flesh" throughout their lives. To me, the DRCs in the last five years have faded past their greatest moments, but for decades they were rich, fleshy, big wines. So was the 1947 Cheval Blanc. So were André's great Beaulieu Vineyard wines.

André drove sports cars, smoked cigarettes, and loved what he did as a winemaker and later in his life as a mentor. He was immensely intuitive about wine. If you wanted to place a bet on which wine would age or where to plant a vineyard, my money was always on André. He introduced the Chappellets to Pritchard Hill, helped the Jordans plant their first vineyard in Sonoma. He knew the secret sauce, "flesh," but he couldn't duplicate it every year. None of us can. We try, we know the goal, we keep our eyes open when the field opens up, and we have a shot. We know it when we taste it.

ROBERT MONDAVI: NAPA VALLEY'S SPOKESMAN

Bob Mondavi was a force of nature. Hard to describe him otherwise. He walked into a room, and there was Mr. Mondavi, or Bob to his friends.

He was happy leading the charge. No, he was happiest leading the charge. He was *the* charge for several decades in Napa Valley, the face of the valley to the world outside. Being the valley's voice pushed all his buttons and put the place on the international wine map. Oh, yes, hundreds of fellow vintners also contributed greatly to the cause, but Bob was the general often in charge. He knew it, and so did we. Right man, right place, maybe more so in retrospect. The legend grows.

He envisioned the Napa Valley Wine Auction, inspired by other charity wine auctions in Europe, like the Hospices de Beaune. As Beringer's representative, I sat in the first steering committee, meeting with a handful of other vintners, and mapped out our first auction, then served on the founding board for this auction. Bob asked me to write the first press release announcing the auction. I did as asked. It was short. We were off to the races.

The first auction taught us much by the mistakes we made. It was far too long, with hundreds of auction items, buckets of food and wine on a scorching day, under a tent that trapped the hot air. We moved around, some napped, put ice cubes in our wine, but we made history. Decades later, fewer lots, Oscar-night audiovisuals, big-time showtime, an immensely successful fundraising machine for important local charities.

The auction evolved, but no one—not even Bob—predicted that it would eventually contribute over $200 million to the health care, education, and charitable support systems within Napa Valley. It, like Bob, grew to be a force of nature with more working parts, a whirlwind of thousands upon thousands of volunteer hours, millions upon millions of vintner dollars, and even more vintner sweat equity. It is a party that attracted wealth and glamour, movie and music industry stars, celebrity chefs, and gained an international reputation for its glitzy parties, its big tent, and the Hollywood-production live auction. Explosions erupted, and sparkling wine corks and glitter flew when the bidding went into the millions, which it often did.

In 2020, this all changed. COVID-19 shut every winery's doors to the world, and the auction went silent. This gave the organizers, the Napa Valley Vintners Association, time to reassess Auction Napa Valley and examine ways to be more inclusive and reach out to a broader audience. It was decided to no longer promote a lavish live auction, but instead create several events, many of them through online programming, to promote Napa Valley, its people, and their wines.

But in 1997, the live auction was in full bloom. That year, I served once again on the steering committee for the auction, and assigned the vintner point person overseeing Lot 007, which was donated by a group of investors whose daytime jobs were producing and distributing the James Bond movies. And, like so many others wanting a piece of Mondavi's "good life," they had invested in a winery. Their plan was to load up the hot new BMW James drove in the film that year with cases of their wine as their donation lot. I presented this idea to the committee, but in those days, there was a movement against lots that included expensive, lavish travel, or cars, yachts, or anything not first and foremost Napa wine–centric. So, the car didn't make the cut. We went back to the drawing board and they devised a fancy Bond gadget–like table filled with wine. M, Bond's gadget maker, would have approved. Secret doors, pop-up bottles of wine, all kinds of working parts. Might have cost as much as the car by the time they were done.

We had a special lot, but what it needed most was a special introduction. The committee decided that I should walk to the stage dressed as Bond and announce myself, "Bond, James Bond." Somehow, I did not feel I was right for the part. Only one person was: Robert Mondavi. I called Bob, and his wife, Margrit, answered. Bob was in a wine tasting, but she promised to discuss it with him and get right back. She called within the hour: "Bob's doing it."

When he walked up to the microphone and announced, "I'm Bond,

Making good wine is a skill, fine wine an art.

—ROBERT MONDAVI, 1913–2008

James Bond," the crowd went nuts, and I truly feel Bob had one of his happiest auction moments that night. "James Bond" had found an Italian suit to wear, and it fit very nicely, thank you. Bob loved to dress up, be the center of attention, and maybe occasionally felt that, in some ways, he was James Bond. He was certainly a man of intrigue and enjoyed the company of women who were attracted to his flair.

A lot of us who worked alongside Bob on committees and boards for long periods of time knew he was a brilliant marketing man and a visionary—and, some thought, a self-promoter. As one might imagine, some of his peers often sensed he was promoting Bob first, then his wineries, Napa Valley, and the "good life," as he put it, in that order. However, if you spent a lot of time working with him, a larger picture emerged, a broader vision of the man. He started solo, breaking from the family business in 1966, to build his own winery, small and very focused. He was going to make wines that would challenge any wine made in any other place in the world. Bordeaux, Burgundy, Champagne, Tuscany—wherever the greatest wines had history and international market share. He wanted Napa Valley to have its own history to tell the world—and definitely a larger piece of the international wine market pie.

Mondavi had grown to ten million cases when Bob was forced to sell the winery in 2004 for $1 billion, including debt. In 1968, they had crushed five hundred tons, or about thirty thousand cases. Over the last two decades before the sale, Mondavi had launched new brands that carried his name: Robert Mondavi Private Selection and Mondavi/Woodbridge, supermarket megabrands made with grapes grown outside Napa Valley, and I sensed the discomfort in Bob with some of the directions his family business had taken. With the increased production and increased number of brands, the name Robert Mondavi had grown bigger. It was a double-edged sword for Bob, but I think he would have given up much of the fame if it meant not feeling forced to take the company public in 1993.

After spending much time working in industry committees and boards with Bob, I sensed that he was losing control of his initial vision—solely a world-class premium brand with an international reputation for only the best. Family members were not at all in agreement on what the future of the winery should be, and there was infighting, which took a toll on all of them. To outsiders, Bob took it stoically, but he was wounded.

During this same period, I watched him privately and publicly encourage and support new, small wineries just getting into the business and help dreamers find their way into the Napa Valley mix. He knew they were essential to the message that Napa Valley could produce world-class wines.

A toast with Robert Mondavi and his winery: (left to right) Ann Colgin, Tor, Walt Klenz (president of Beringer), Julia Child, and Robert Mondavi

I watched and realized it was not really all about Bob. It was about Napa Valley's place in the hierarchy of international wines. He partnered with Château Mouton Rothschild, the Baroness, and the Rothschild family, and later with the Frescobaldi family in Italy. Napa Valley was an equal, not a New World upstart.

I cannot count the times I heard Bob stand up and repeat himself, over and over again. At industry gatherings, small or very large, like *Wine Spectator*'s New York Wine Experience, winery representatives would mouth the speech before Bob said the first word. They knew it by heart. And they knew Bob would be the first man to stand up to make his point.

"Napa Valley makes world-class wines that stand up against anything out there. Napa Valley makes world-class wines . . ." Yes, he grew repetitive, but he was highly effective. Just look at his legend—it grows larger by the day. Without Bob Mondavi, Napa would be recognized on the world's stage but not to the extent it is today. He put the pedal to the metal.

I was in a New York taxi with wine writer James Laube after one New York Wine Experience tasting, and on the corner, we saw Bob and Margrit

Robert Mondavi and the Baroness Philippine de Rothschild launching Opus One

trying to hail a cab. They didn't have the full-time limo on call. They were having a difficult time, and we managed to pull over and make room for them in our cab. Bob talked about the greatness of Napa Valley until we reached their restaurant in the Village, close to ours. He stayed on script, and James and I loved every minute, even though we had seen the film many times before.

LEADING THE CHARGE

Through the eighties and nineties, Bob would select a dozen or more employees each year—all devout, loyal champions of the winery—and show them Europe's culinary and winery shrines through his eyes. France and Italy carried the day, and many of the lucky employees who boarded those planes and buses saw Bob in his raw element: leading the charge, enjoying the "good life" with his soldiers.

One of the winery's well-known tour guides (some were celebrities in their own right) told me that few of the youngest in his group couldn't keep up with Bob, and they had to devise ways to slow him down. One strategy was to privately tip a waiter at each restaurant to keep Bob's glass filled throughout the long meals. Even then, he left those half or one-third his age gasping for air. I heard a writer ask him how much he drank each day, and he replied, a bit unsure, "A bottle?" I sensed he thought this was a safe answer, being on the low side. He liked his wine. Great wines and meals fueled the tank that ran his unstoppable engine. "The good life."

The multimillion-dollar failure Copia, the Center for Wine, Food, and the Arts, was his and Margrit's dream. Possibly ahead of its time, it failed for a number of reasons: art was on equal display with wine and food, and some argued it was even more prominent. Its downtown Napa location was difficult for tourists to get to during its start-up years. And, perhaps more important, it did not appeal to most tourists coming to Napa Valley. They wanted what had driven tourism in the valley the last two decades: tasting experiences—emphasis on *experiences*—as well as memorable dining experiences. This includes wine-and-food pairings, themed wineries (castles, palaces, architectural monuments), and Michelin-starred restaurants. Many tourists did not want to spend their day at an art museum.

Julia Child knew that the Copia vision was a hard sell, and we often talked about this. She asked me to join the Copia board, and I did. Saying no to Julia was not in my vocabulary. We watched them build Copia for $70 million, name the restaurant after Julia (she was very reluctant on this), and struggle from the beginning to make it work. It plunged into debt, and a few board members rescued it briefly with a bond issue, but its fate seemed sealed from the beginning.

That said, Bob asked me to join him on a Mondavi private aircraft one day to fly up to Seattle for lunch with Howard Schultz, founder and president of Starbucks. Bob and I were the only passengers, so I had a lot of private time with him. Most of our time previously had been in a full room or board meetings, lunches at Copia and the Mondavi winery, American Institute of Wine & Food (AIWF) events, dinners with Julia and others. Sadly, our conversations that day were not very revealing. They did not stray to family matters or the world outside the wine business. We stayed on the subject of our meeting—how could we get Howard Schultz on board to contribute a serious donation to Copia?

We had our lunch at the Starbucks headquarters in south Seattle. Sandwiches in a private room, cookies for dessert. No wine, no multiple courses of food paired to a different wine, very unlike Bob's normal working lunch. Howard, I learned, was a huge Robert Mondavi fan. He started the meeting by setting that point in stone. He had closely observed Bob's brilliant marketing of the Mondavi brand from the beginning—especially the font and illustration of the winery entrance that still adorns the label today. He said it inspired the Starbucks logo and the use of it on all marketing material. He was not a big fan of the wines, but he was a fan of the man and the brand he had built. He did not contribute to Copia, but that might have been because I am not a very good salesman. Bob certainly was. As was Howard Schultz, I might add. I bought stock in Starbucks after our lunch that day, and it has turned out to be one of my most profitable stock picks. Thank you, Howard.

From the beginning, Bob Mondavi introduced the world to Napa Valley. We almost take it for granted today. He unveiled our first emblems of the good life—cooking schools, barrel tastings, experiential wine tastings, extensive wine education programing, live winery concert series, Fumé Blanc, weird packaging, blind wine tastings with the First Growths. The list goes on. There were mistakes (some weird bottle shapes and closures that came and went) and some grand slam out-of-the-park successes along the way. I remember those successes and have forgotten the rest—except Copia.

Copia, along with another multimillion philanthropic pledge to the University of California at Davis, proved to be a fatal Achilles' heel for Bob and the Mondavi winery. In excess of $40 million had been pledged in the way of stock in the Mondavi public company, and when the stock plunged, Bob's pledges put him in a dangerous financial position. Bankruptcy seemed imminent if the stock continued to fall. In the bloody end, Bob and his family were forced to take Constellation's $1 billion offer for the winery and the winery brands, the Mondavi name on a wine, and 50 percent of Opus One, his joint venture with the Mouton Rothschilds. His eponymous winery was now irrevocably in another's hand. The General was asked to be a symbol, beloved but no longer the man leading the charge.

The last time I saw Bob alive, the years, the battles, the wins, and the defeats had taken their toll. He was in a wheelchair, not speaking much, not in full charge of his mind, and hard of hearing. He had what Julia had once called "the dwindles," something her beloved husband had suffered from at the end of his life. Bob was in his nineties and still Napa's icon, recognizable to most everyone whose path crossed his. The location was of one of Thomas Keller's restaurants, Ad Hoc, and Bob was with Margrit, some family, and close friends.

On the last day we saw them together, my wife, Susan, and I went over to say hello. We knew most of the group. When we were reintroduced, Bob looked at me very intently. I have no idea what he was thinking, but it was one of Bob's forceful, focused stares. I was the only person in the room for that long moment. He never uttered a word; he just stared at me. Finally, everyone but Bob smiled and said goodbye, and he was wheeled to the large table awaiting them.

Every person in the restaurant that day knew that Robert Mondavi was in attendance. He was the man, the legend. He will probably be thought of in my lifetime, maybe for all time, as America's greatest winemaker and vintner. He worked hard dedicating a lifetime to his prominent place in our history. A lot of us were lucky to know him and work with him.

When I pass the Mondavi winery, I think of all the lunches, seminars, concerts, and meetings I attended in the back of the building looking out at the Mayacamas Mountains. The very symbol of the winery is the entrance, with its nod to the California missions, yet with more graceful and modern lines. The tour guides are still top-notch, excellent educators and rock stars of their trade. The tastings are worth every penny, although they cost a few more than they did when Bob opened the doors in 1966. I invite you to take a tour and hear the story of a man, of a dream, of a great American winery. The top wines are still great and would make Bob proud.

Bob's greatest legacy might not be discussed often. It was how he opened up his winery as a training ground right from the beginning. Over the decades, numerous winemakers, CEOs, COOs, and wine-industry leaders worked at Robert Mondavi Winery, cutting their teeth and pursuing their own dreams. Helen Turley began her extraordinary career in the Mondavi lab. Warren Winiarski, Mike Grgich, Paul Hobbs, and Zelma Long all began their wine careers working for Bob.

The name *Mondavi* on a résumé was golden. The winery attracted the best and the brightest, and Bob encouraged and nurtured their entrepreneurial spirit. He had an ego and a large heart for anyone who wanted to work hard to pursue their dreams. In my mind, a fitting tribute to Robert Mondavi would be a wall at the winery inscribed with the names of all the industry greats whose careers were launched there. A true testament to a complicated but born ambassador for wine and "the good life."

A meal without wine is like a day without sunshine.

—JEAN ANTHELME BRILLAT-SAVARIN
FRENCH LAWYER, POLITICIAN, AND WRITER, 1755–1826

MARCH

MY GEARS START SWITCHING, nerves begin twitching in March. The climb begins, the heartbeats accelerate, and views of all that needs to be accomplished for another year open up. Tastings accelerate at the winery with my winemaker. We can compare two vintages with an open dialogue—which barrels performed best, which vintage has more weight, early perfume, and more.

It is time to bottle the Chardonnays from the vintage before last unless we feel more barrel age might improve the wines. We rack the wine from their barrels into tanks to sit and settle for a month so we can bottle unfiltered, which is time-consuming and expensive, but worth it. I believe 99 percent of all wines are filtered in some way, so this is uncommon. Why do we do it? I think there is more stuffing, more solids, more of what wine can be with less filtration. Why are most wines filtered? It is the safe road to take; you've created a sterile, clean environment for the wine. You don't have to worry about anything waking up and creating problems down the road. We run all the tests we need to make sure we can bottle unfiltered. Worth all the time and expense.

Bottling is my least favorite time of year. Murphy's Law—if anything can go wrong, it very well might—rules the day. You have to be buttoned up to get through years of bottling. The labels, glass, corks, and capsules all must be there, and have to fit. No margin of error is acceptable. I open a good wine when I get through a bottling day without issues and celebrate. I open a good bottle when I do have issues and battle through them. I might need it more on those days—to pause, catch my breath, and know that I'm done for another year. I told you I hate bottling.

Budbreak begins in earnest in the vineyards. The days are lengthening, warming, and the young vines awaken. Frost damage is still a threat. Palissage, or trellising repair work, continues, as does the pruning. The valleys and hillsides are green. Mustard lines the rows of vines in many of the vineyards. To me, March is one of the most beautiful months of the year in Napa Valley if it is not raining a lot. We need the rain this month, but I do love the blue sky and buttermilk clouds framed with greens and yellows. The crisp, clean air tastes and smells like anything is possible.

JULIA CHILD's ITINERARY

Wednesday, December 8th

11:01 AM Pick up at United Airlines terminal SFO.
12:30 PM Back in the Napa Valley (lunch?)
        Check in at Villagio Inn & Spa (21797)
5 PM We will leave for a reception for American Center Trustees at the home of Richard and Monene Bradley in St. Helena. (transportation tbd)
5:30-7:30 PM Reception at the Bradleys'
7:15 PM You and Anne Willan leave for dinner at the French Laundry. Toni Allegra will meet you there.

Thursday, December 9th

9 AM The Trustees meeting for the American Center will be at the Robert Mondavi Winery. The meeting will begin at 9, with coffee at 8:30. You may want to ride up with Anne, or we will arrange transportation for you. Lunch will be served at noon. Annie Bennett who has been President of our board is retiring and Joe Wender is becoming President, and so there will be some festivities.
2PM I will take you back to the Center office in Napa and show you our detailed plans and models for all aspects of the Center. We can also go by the construction site so you can see our progress. It is very exciting!
4PM We will take you back to Villagio, where you have some free time.
7PM Peggy Loar and Kevin Crain will pick you up and take you to Terra in St Helena for dinner. Alan Simon (my sweetie) and I will join you there. We are planning a very festive evening. Peggy and Kevin will take you back to Villagio afterwards.

Friday, December 10th

9:30 AM Tor will pick you up and bring you to Meadowood Resort to check in
5:45 PM Tor will pick you up for the reception at the Martini's home – then you will have dinner at Brix

Saturday, December 11th

AM??? If you are free in the morning, Daphne can arrange a kitchen tour at Meadowood for you.
12:00 PM Bob and Margrit Mondavi will pick you up for lunch.
12:30 PM Reservations at Bistro Jeante.
PM??? Bob and Margrit have invited you to join them in the Robert Mondavi Vineyard Room for the winery's sit-down dinner Christmas party. Please call Julie Prince, Margrit's assistant ((707) 968-2203), she is hoping to hear from you.

Sunday, December 12th

11:15 AM Tor will pick you up
11:30 Lunch at Pinot Blanc with Tor Kenward   *ok? (they can keep her busy)*
6:15 PM Tor will pick you up at Meadowood
6:30 PM Auction Dinner fulfillment at Hudson House

Julia's more detailed itinerary for one of her Napa trips

With those Napa Valley images in mind, this is a good time to introduce three wonderful women who chartered the direction of my life significantly: my wife, Susan; Belle (and Barney) Rhodes; and Julia Child. Their lives and mine intertwined over a few decades, with more rich and colorful stories than I have space to tell. But I can share some good ones with you here.

FOREVER JULIA

The learning curve for both winemakers and chefs is endless, so curiosity makes the cat. You might tire of me saying this. Julia Child helped me understand that fact of life over the years we had as friends. We never know it all as winemakers or chefs. There will always be more to learn about our professions if we stay curious and passionate about these fields of endeavor. Julia was always interested in who was new and what they were thinking and doing in the kitchen. She loved her wines as much as a good cocktail, but I think she enjoyed young and passionate winemakers more than the wine they made.

Julia cared about all practicing restaurant chefs she met. If we were out to dinner, she would never leave without going into their kitchens and asking them questions about what they were preparing, what interested them. She was sincerely curious. She was always asking questions; I cannot remember her offering direction. She appeared to be constantly learning, a youthful person up to her death.

I met Julia in the 1980s, the early days of the American Institute of Wine & Food (AIWF). I had built several successful culinary programs at Beringer and established the School for American Chefs with the brilliant Madeleine Kamman. Julia and I crossed paths frequently. She asked me to join the national board for the AIWF, which I did, staying on for a decade (my limit for a board). She then asked me to join the board of Copia, the Center for Wine, Food, and Arts, which she cared deeply about, and which was spearheaded by Bob and Margrit Mondavi. Again, I said yes and stayed for another eight years.

I don't think I ever said no to Julia. I felt that if I did, I would miss something important. And because of this, I have many fond memories. In 1992, I was asked to chair a dinner and AIWF auction celebrating her eightieth birthday at the Hay-Adams hotel in Washington, DC, and consequently two other annual AIWF auctions she attended and supported. I always felt at a loss for words when introducing her, most likely because she needed no introduction. So, I kept opening remarks short—the audience wanted to hear Julia.

I remember one time, we jumped on an elevator at the World Trade Center, and as the elevator filled, everyone's eyes were on her. A teenager in the elevator blurted out to his friends, "That's Julia Child." Everyone else knew that, but he was just a teenager. I always wondered if he secretly watched the reruns of her cooking show. She was an icon who transcended generations.

In her later years, I had the honor to escort her around Napa Valley, driving her to various meetings, dinners, and lunches. Even as I began to wane, she would still be going strong into the night, asking questions, curious, and enjoying the company of others. She said she lived on small naps, never long hours of sleep, but I think she lived on being in the company of others who shared her passions: all things dealing with good food, people, and politics.

Yes, she was very liberal, so different from her conservative parents from Pasadena, California. She often talked about how different her life would have been if she had not traveled to France and fallen in love. There was her husband, Paul, and all the fabulous food. And, I should add, she loved butter and would make sure I ate my proper amount when we dined together. Lean cuisine was an oxymoron or just plain blasphemy. She knew where the real flavors lurked.

Oh, and she had a devilish sense of humor, dry and laser like. Heaven help the self-righteous or strongly opinionated chef who might invite a quick jab. One very well-known chef once told her he used only ingredients that were fresh, local, and in season. She told him nicely, "That is silly. We have airplanes and the world is full of good food. Why not share it when it is needed?" When asked her opinion of Jerusalem artichokes, she summarized, "Wonderful for flatulence."

LUNCH WITH JULIA

Once, when I picked her up at Meadowood in St. Helena, where she often stayed, I had to do a little domestic business before we took off for lunch with some important people Julia had to meet that day. It was a working lunch to expand the donor base for Copia. My wife, Susan, was back east visiting friends, and I was managing my eleven-year-old son's days during summer break. Cooper was sleeping in when I left the house, and he needed waking and to know what I had cooked for him and where it was.

I had a speaker in the car, got him on the phone, and started with my brief instructions. Once Julia sized up my situation, she nicely asked, "Cooper, can you join us for lunch?" There was a long pause at both ends.

It was my turn. "Cooper, Julia's invited you to join us if you're up to it. Would you like to come?"

"Yes," was the reply. He was earnest, interested.

"Then quickly put on some khakis and a dress shirt, and we'll pick you up in five minutes."

Julia and I together in the Copia kitchen

HOW LONG SHOULD WINE AGE BEFORE I DRINK IT?

The answer is right now or any time after, up to a point. Getting to know your own "point" is the secret. No two people share the same point. Some like their wines with a lot of age. Most don't. Most of the wine consumed in America is aged on a car seat from the supermarket to the dinner table or hot tub.

He was ready when we got there and carried on a very good conversation with Julia on the drive. I was a very proud father. With Julia's urging, he sat next to her during the multicourse lunch. Every chef wanted to show off, and long multicourse meals were part of Julia's life on the road. That day, Julia talked as much to Cooper as she did to any of our other lunch guests, or so it seemed to me. She was sincerely interested in what he was interested in, what food he liked, and what he wanted to do. It was an enchanting lunch he never forgot, nor did I.

Several years later, Susan and I were in the Sierra Nevada on an escape vacation, away from TV and the world. One morning, Cooper called. His voice and demeanor when I answered were very serious, which immediately concerned us.

"Dad, I don't know if you have heard yet," he said. "Julia has passed away." We talked about her, and I reminded him of how many people she had touched in her lifetime. I really didn't need to do this and quickly realized in a short period of time she had made a huge and lasting impression on him. He was like so many others whose lives were changed in small and large ways by her interest in who they were and what they did.

When I talk to groups, I mention my past and present mentors. Winemakers like André Tchelistcheff, my good friend Myron Nightingale, Bob Mondavi, and so many others in the early days. Now I listen to my winemaker, Jeff Ames, and his peers, Andy Erickson, Thomas Brown, and so many others, far younger but still curious. We share information on winemaking. We ask questions. We get answers. We share more information. Some people seemed surprised that, after five decades as a student of wine, I am still a student and relish discovery. Winemaking is also winegrowing; it is science and art; it is constantly changing, shifting, trying to keep us off balance, or lead us down another rabbit hole.

During the last five decades, I have run into wine professionals who are very fixed in their ideas about wine. They act as if they know most all there is to know, and their opinions are narrow. Most in this group have been a

Julia's eightieth birthday at the Hay-Adams in Washington,
DC, 1992: (left to right) Warren Winiarski (winemaker),
Tor (chair for the formal celebration), Roger Berkowitz (CEO
of Legal Sea Foods), and Julia

wine professional (or amateur) for less than a decade. If I run into them ten years later, they know far less, unless they have taken up another hobby to be an expert in.

Julia, thank you for inspiring me to continue learning, growing, and challenging myself. You wrote books that changed the American kitchen forever. You entertained us on TV, making it okay to be a cook who makes mistakes. You inspired me to be curious. It remains in my top five most important lessons in life. Don't ask me about the other four. I'm still forming an opinion.

FIRST DATE AT THE RHODESES'

I'm not big on gossip. My wife is, but she's a Southern girl from Richmond, Virginia, where gossip flows more freely than mint juleps on a warm summer day. Reverence for gossip seems wired by your upbringing. All that said, gossip season is in full swing by May. We live in a small valley, in a small town. Word gets around fast when the wine cellars open and the neighbors arrive.

My first date with Susan was at the home of Belle and Barney Rhodes. Through the seventies, eighties, and into the nineties, their home in Rutherford was the equivalent of Gertrude Stein's salon in Paris between the world wars. However, art was not what they collected. They collected wine and cookbooks and brought to their salon writers, chefs, and winemakers from all over the world. My wife had written several successful cookbooks before we met, and Belle had them in her library.

You never turned down an invitation for dinner at their home. If you did, you might miss meeting someone who could change your life. I met writers like Michael Broadbent, Master of Wine (MW), and Harry Waugh; winemakers from France, Italy, Spain, and Napa; and celebrity chefs from all over the world, and new ones arriving to make Napa their home. I have said on many occasions that Belle and Barney were my surrogate parents in Napa Valley. Quietly, and in their own gentle way, they nurtured my love of wine and food, and I owe them a lot. They did not seek fame or social status. They sought friendships and a full table of interesting people who loved food and wine, polite gossip and conversation.

Belle was a matchmaker. If a vintner was looking for vineyards, you would be seated next to the grape grower who could change the direction of your life. If you were a young chef arriving in Napa Valley, you were seated next to the people who would help you on a road to success. Just ask Thomas Keller, Cindy Pawlcyn, or Michael Chiarello. A winemaker like me, might be seated next to other winemakers: Warren Winiarski, Bob

Mondavi, André Tchelistcheff, or a walking encyclopedia of wine and food like Darrell Corti. The wines were carefully choreographed by Barney. They were impeccable bottles from all over the world, curated to stimulate conversation. Barney's cellar was as deep as any I've ever walked into. It was a well-curated history vault of California wine and all the greatest hits from the Old World—heavy in Bordeaux and Port.

On one of these wild and crazy nights, the topic of false rumors came up. It was a very sore subject to the winemakers in the room that night—that California wines don't age. All show, no go. Now, you should remember that this was a decade after the 1976 Paris Wine Tasting, and this *faux bruit* was quite literally blown out of the water. If you don't know about the Paris Wine Tasting of 1976, here's what happened in a nutshell.

In a blind tasting in Paris, the best and brightest European palates voted

Tor and Bella Rhodes turn their attention to the photographer during one of our many dinner parties.

a Napa Cabernet Sauvignon and a Napa Valley Chardonnay the number one wines. They had no idea what they were tasting, but they sure liked the California wines, confused them with French wines—and wanted their score cards back and burned. Thank goodness a journalist from *Time* magazine, George Taber, was in the room and published the story. The rest is history, and over the decades, when memories seem to fade, we do it again, with close to the same results.

Yet the rumor stays out there in dark corners. In the eighties, it was very persistent on the East Coast, particularly in the New York wine trade. When you think about it, it is easy to understand: we were the new kids on the block, and we had an attitude. Bordeaux and Burgundy had deep roots in the Big Apple, and they did not want to share that sweet fruit with the new kids. Very understandable in retrospect, but that night at Belle and Barney's, we were drinking very good wine, and we were riled up.

I must have been seriously enjoying the wines that evening, for I volunteered to call the wine writer for the *New York Times*, Frank Prial, the next day and invite him out to Napa. We'd prove once and for all to all the New York uninformed wine snobs that we made wines that aged incredibly well—in fact, maybe better than their old-world counterparts. Yep, we'd prove them, all right. Belle and Barney had the ammo for this attack in their wine cellar. Prial, many in the room felt, had a bias for French wine. One called him Franco-Prial. It was war, and I volunteered for the first wave.

The next morning, I found less courage for my charge into battle but did manage to pick up the phone and call the *New York Times*. They put me right through. I think this is a good time to give him the narrative. He wrote a very lengthy piece in the *New York Times Magazine* about what happened next. Mr. Prial, the podium is yours.

CALIFORNIA, HERE I COME

It started with a telephone call. A fellow from St. Helena, a little town in California's Napa Valley, rang me up some time back. "We're going to have an interesting dinner," he said, "and we'd like you to come."

"But," I replied, "I'm in New York and you're 3,000 miles away."

"Well," he said, "we're going to open some interesting wines." And then he read me this list:

1969 Schramsberg Blanc de Noirs. 1968 Souverain Johannisberg Riesling. 1971 Heitz Cellar Johannisberg Riesling. 1965 Heitz Cellar Pinot Blanc. 1967 Heitz Cellar Pinot Blanc. 1969 Heitz Cellar Pinot Blanc. 1965 Stony Hill Chardonnay. 1967 Stony Hill Chardonnay. 1961 Heitz Cellar Pinot Chardonnay. 1962 Heitz Cellar Pinot Chardonnay. 1951 Louis M. Martini Cabernet Sauvignon. 1951 Beaulieu Vineyard Cabernet Private Reserve Georges de Latour. 1952 Beaulieu Vineyard Cabernet Private Reserve Georges de Latour. 1952 Louis M. Martini Cabernet Sauvignon. 1958 Inglenook Vineyard Cabernet Sauvignon Cask F11. 1958 Charles Krug Cabernet Sauvignon. 1958 Beaulieu Vineyard Private Reserve Georges de Latour. 1949 Inglenook Vineyard Pinot Noir. 1955 Beaulieu Vineyard Pinot Noir. 1958 Hanzell Vineyards Pinot Noir. 1959 Heitz Cellar Pinot Noir. 1960 Heitz Cellar Pinot Noir. 1973 Wente Bros. Riesling Auslese. 1973 Freemark Abbey Edelwein. 1960 (circa) Cresta Blanca Premier Semillon. 1953 Ficklin Vineyards Port.

"I'll be there," I said, and I was, along with a dozen or so assorted wine makers, writers, collectors and other delicate snouts—what the French call fines gueules. After all, how often does an invitation come along to a dinner with 26 famous California wines from memorable vintages, some of them at least 30 years old and most of them destined never to be seen or tasted again. These wines came from the cellars of three friends, Dr. Bernard Rhodes, Bob Thompson and Dr. Bob Adamson, who are more than just avid collectors; all have grown up with California wines and have lived the history of each bottle they open.

The man who called me was Tor Kenward, a Beringer Vineyards' executive, who had offered Rhine House, the old Beringer mansion in St. Helena, for the evening, along with Beringer's young chef, Gary J. Danko.

Dr. Rhodes recently retired as director of the Kaiser Health Plan and Hospitals, and once owned the land on which the famous Martha's Vineyard cabernet sauvignon is grown, and Bob Thompson is one of California's foremost wine writers. So immersed are they in their subject that they could recall just about every vintage we sampled; the frost in the spring of one year, the hot summer days in another, the unexpected rain during the harvest in a third.

They knew, too, that Heitz Cellar's 1961 and 1962 chardonnays—still called pinot chardonnay in those days—came from Hanzell Vineyards, over in Sonoma, the winery started by James D. Zellerbach, former United States Ambassador to Italy. Mr. Zellerbach built Hanzell to duplicate the wines he had grown to love in France. When he died, the winery was closed down for a time and its wines, many still aging in barrels, were sold off. Mr. Heitz bought the chardonnay and finished it in his own style.

They explained, too, how many of the Heitz pinot blanc grapes came from Fred McCrea's vineyards at Stony Hill, in the rugged hills northwest of here. If Joe Heitz became something of a legend for his great cabernets, Mr. McCrea holds a similar title for his chardonnays. He made great chardonnays at Stony Hill when experts were still saying California could never produce good white wines. Thanks to Mr. McCrea and a few others like him, chardonnay

Barney Rhodes, Tor, Narsai David (restaurateur/wine collector) celebrating Barney's birthday

eventually eclipsed pinot blanc and other white grapes as the source of California's premier white wine.

If anything distinguished the white wines at the dinner, it was their freshness and youth. Long years in the bottle had added delightful complexity and hardly a hint of oxidation. It would be rare to find a similar group of white Burgundies that had held up as well. I found the 1965 Stony Hill and the 1962 Heitz to be a couple of the best.

The stars of the dinner were, as they usually are, the cabernet sauvignons. If the list sounds as if the hosts had obeyed Captain Renault's instructions in Casablanca *to "round up the usual suspects," it must be remembered that in the 1950s there really were only a handful of serious wineries in California. After Charles Krug, Louis Martini, Inglenook and Beaulieu, it was mostly jug wine.*

What is remarkable about those years—and what this particular dinner showed once again—is the way these four wineries, with a very small market to serve, turned out exceptional wines year after year. It's also interesting to recall that most of these wines originally sold for $2, more or less, a bottle. My own favorites were the 1951 and 1958 Beaulieu Private Reserve, and the 1952 Martini and the 1958 Charles Krug.

Oh yes, with these wines, we ate:

Salmon medallion, with leeks, cabbage and two caviars. Truffled foie gras and sweetbread terrine. Peking duck breast salad with glazed turnips, pears, and pearl onions. Noisettes of lamb with fennel compote and tarragon lamb essence. Mushrooms, snails, and air-dried beef on croutons. Baked raspberries in lemon cream. Port sherbert with flakes of Stilton cheese and pistachios.

Thank you, Belle and Barney. We miss you. We miss dinner parties that go deep into the night, our consciousness, and our memories. You brought out the best in us, nurtured this crazy kid, and helped shape my life. Susan and I survived our first date at your home and have two wonderful kids to remind us. You're not world famous, but you did more for Napa Valley than most anyone I know during our formative years. You will always be celebrated in the hearts of all those you touched.

Give me books, fruit, French wine and fine weather, and a little music out of doors, played by somebody I do not know.

—JOHN KEATS
ENGLISH POET, 1795–1821

APRIL

I WAS BORN IN APRIL, so I have an affinity for the month. Triple Aries, whatever that means. I think of April, and I think it is time to socialize, to get out of the winery more and share wines. As a winemaker, you make wine, and you have to sell it, or you will be forced to retire very early. April is a good month to open your wines, share them, and sell them. It is also a good month to hit the road and explore other wine-growing regions, sit down with other winemakers and winegrowers, and exchange information.

At the winery, we continue to work on blends for June bottlings of the Cabernets and the red wine blends. In the vineyard, there is still a hint of frost in the air as the young, green shoots take off, and the tendrils search for a grip on the trellising. Most modern vineyards are trained in vertical shoot positioning, or VSP. Simply put, we and our wiring systems encourage the young, green plant material to shoot for the stars in a way that causes the young clusters to line up in a zone where they are exposed to direct sunlight for periods of the day and more easily accessible by a picker's hand when it comes time to harvest. This method of training a vine and positioning the fruit has changed modern wines as much as advances in modern winemaking equipment. There is more uniformity to the quality and ripeness of the clusters.

When I arrived in Napa Valley in the 1970s, most vineyards were head-, cane-, or cordon-trained in what we called California sprawl. The result was many exposed clusters that were ripe to overripe and others that were heavily shaded and underripe. The results were wines that often had a distinct green or overripe flavor, or somehow both. Some people are fans of this; I'm less so, except in rare cases with head-trained, older vines where the clusters might need more sun protection than exposure and the roots are deep. I have had memorable wines from fifty-plus-year-old vines that were dry farmed and head pruned. Since these were planted, viticulturalists discovered that a little direct sunlight (not a lot) on the clusters softens the tannins in the wines. The wines are less tannic and more round tasting because of how they are grown, not just how they are made. VSP has significantly changed wines in most popular winegrowing regions in the world; though seldom discussed outside industry chat rooms, it is a game changer.

Travel to other growing areas has been a huge part of my wine education and appreciation. When I buy wines from other countries, I remember walking the vineyards and talking with the vignerons, and the wine comes into full sensory focus. Visuals, smells, flavors, and sounds all come together. When I became a full-time vintner in 1977, I proudly applied for my first passport. Since then, I have traveled to most of the major winegrowing regions of the world and lately to world-class fly-fishing destinations. I'm a serial traveler at heart. I have learned far more from these travels than from any classroom, book, lecture, and movie combined. In this chapter, we open the portal to eternal inspiration: travel.

INSPIRATION

Someone asked me to write about my life in lockdown in 2020, which launched this book. I tried to wrap my head around it, and no, I didn't want to dwell on the pluses and minuses of life during a pandemic. In 2020, we had brilliant essays, social media, blogs, and films addressing our loneliness and confusion. Like Tom Hanks's character in the movie *Cast Away* who was isolated with Wilson the volleyball after it washed up on his beach, we shifted and adjusted to isolation. And I started writing. But not about isolation. Quite the opposite.

I wrote about travel, adventure, and getting out into the vibrant, lively world I've been to before, crowded with poets, blue-collar laborers of all professions, lords and ladies, struggling winemakers, and dreamers. I cooked meals that I remembered from my travels, with smells that transported

I LOVE TO TRAVEL
to regions that make their own wines. The food is always outstanding; the people happy, inviting, and memorable.

me to those frozen moments in time with the people I talked to, laughed alongside, and broke bread with and opened wine for around crowded tables. Writing, cooking, and opening wines at home allowed me a way to travel again.

My first trip back into this time machine was to Paris in 1981—my first trip to France and my first trip to Europe as a young man.

I cried when the 747 hit the tarmac at Charles de Gaulle. It was April. I remember it so well—there was still a little snow that hadn't melted on the sides of the runway. When I left Napa Valley for Europe, it was getting hot. In France, it was still a cold, lingering spring and a gray day as I first stepped on French soil. But for me, it didn't matter, because I had been given the keys to the kingdom. The City of Light. My imagination of what my next two weeks would be gave me butterflies. And, yes, I did cry with happiness on that gray morning.

In 1975 and 1976, I camped in the Bothe–Napa Valley State Park to explore wineries in Napa for retail wine shops. I had my jazz club in Southern California, and I lived from concert to concert. Oscar Peterson, Stan Getz, and Chick Corea were a few of the artists we booked. A bohemian life, but I was legitimately broke, living in a former chauffeur's quarters for thirty dollars a month and cooking for those who would and could open the great wines that inspired my move to Napa.

In 1977, I moved permanently to Napa Valley to become a vintner. Beringer had hired me and was sending me to France to sit down with winemakers and château owners to taste, talk, dine, and absorb everything I had only read about in books. I was getting paid to do what I would have easily given every dollar I had to experience, but in 1977, that wouldn't have covered the airfare.

Wine replaced music as the primary focus in my life, transporting me to a world where time disappears, and your feet rarely touch the ground. Napa was my new home, and in the seventies, it was a bit of the Wild West for a new generation of winemakers. The vignerons of France and the historic châteaux and wineries where the legendary wines that had inspired my journey originated, were the establishment. They had class, deep roots, and wisdom—and I would be asking them for their secrets over the next two weeks.

My job at Beringer was to integrate winemaking with marketing, define our reserve programs, write newsletters, and communicate through all channels that we were serious about fine wine. Along with other Napa vintners, we were fighting for respect and swapping out years of mediocre wine for promises of new, world-class Cabernet and Chardonnay. I was in France

WINE IS NOT COMPLICATED

It can even make itself without any help from us. The complications are all ours. We put wine on a pedestal above all other natural beverages. Some embrace these complications and the pedestal. I prefer the dinner table surrounded by good friends who embrace wine's simple enjoyment. It is harder to drink wine off a pedestal.

to learn and to bring to Napa new ideas to make and market fine wine.

Beringer had a subsidiary import company called Crosse & Blackwell Cellars that imported wines from France, Germany, Italy, and Spain, with extraordinary contacts in the European wine trade. There was not one château or winery in Europe that they couldn't get me into: Domaine de la Romanée-Conti, Château Pétrus, Château Latour, Château Mouton Rothschild, Château Margaux—they were all on my list to visit.

I spent my first afternoon and night alone in Paris. Yet I wasn't alone. The smells, the architecture, and the history brought romance to each step. I was in love at first sight with this city and have remained so, returning many times—building a map in my mind of its arrondissements, museums, and restaurants. My best days in Paris have been those with no agenda. Wake up, have coffee and a pastry, and start walking, seeing, and eating. That has never lost its magic.

The restaurants I experienced during that trip to France—in Paris, Bordeaux, Burgundy, Lyon—forever changed my life. I returned to Napa Valley on a mission to elevate our hospitality and our food-and-wine programs at Beringer. Mondavi was beginning to go down the same road, and I was going with him. Julia Child and Robert Mondavi would ask me years later to join their founding boards for AIWF and Copia. It was the right road to travel, and it would change Napa Valley in so many ways over the next four decades.

Today, Napa Valley is internationally known for its food and wines. That was not the case in 1980. There were no destination restaurants or hotels in Napa Valley. Few wineries entertained, and if they did, it was often with a sandwich and the expectation the visitor would be gone by sundown. All this would change quickly, and those days in Paris were shining a light on our yellow brick road.

My first meal in Paris was a simple late lunch at a corner café near my hotel. No Michelin stars. I ordered turbot (a first) with green beans and a bottle of Domaine François Raveneau. The bread was incredible, as was the butter. I watched the people walk by and let time vanish. While I ate, I studied my itinerary and Hugh Johnson's paperback edition of *The World Atlas of Wine*.

The atlas was my only source of maps to locate the wineries and vineyards I would visit. I had road maps, but no other way to find a winery or a vineyard other than what Hugh gave me. GPS—really? Years later, Hugh and I had dinner together when he was promoting a new book. I presented my old beaten-up paperback edition, which had been on my lap for so many miles throughout Europe, for him to sign, which he did, along with a new edition. We had some good laughs. I buy each new edition that comes out—up to eight, signed by the brilliant coauthor, my friend Jancis Robinson, MW.

As I turned the pages that featured places I would soon visit, I realized I needed to wake up early, rent a car, and drive to Épernay. My first visit was the great, historic Champagne house and home of Dom Pérignon, Moët & Chandon. As I sipped my Chablis and turned pages, I worked on my French, praying I could drive in a foreign country without killing anyone or destroying the car. A friend in Napa, the GM at Moët & Chandon, had made the introduction, and I realized I had no idea what to expect, only that I would spend the night as Moët's guest. Nothing else. After my visit to Champagne, my schedule was set. Tomorrow was mostly a mystery of expectations.

A CHANGED MAN

I rented a loaded Peugeot 405 the next day from an agency near the hotel and launched into morning Paris traffic. The sun was out as I gripped the steering wheel, maneuvering through the roundabouts with two maps on my lap. I was not cautious, constantly glancing at the maps while driving. Nor should anyone dare drive near me. Nevertheless, I made it to Épernay without incident around midday and found the bustling tourist center at Moët & Chandon.

Somehow, someway, I found someone who was expecting me. I was quite content to join the regular tour that was leaving the reception area, but I was ushered off to another room. There's no other way to summarize what happened during the next twenty-four hours other than to say that it changed my life.

I was introduced to one of the Moët winemakers, whose English was better than my French. He gave me a personal, abbreviated tour of the cellars,

SHOULD I DECANT MY WINE?

A little air should help all well-made wines, red and white. The bigger question: do you like cleaning decanters? I don't, but I use them when they are really needed. This is usually for a very young red wine, to give it a lot of air quickly, or a very old red wine, to remove the wine from the sediment it might have thrown off over time. Sit the latter up several days before. A nice wineglass is a wonderful way to give wine the air it needs in most cases. Work it. And you won't have to clean a decanter.

the largest underground cellar in Champagne, with 17 miles (28 kilometers) of tunnels. We did not get lost. We made the usual tourist stops: Caveau Napoleon, where the emperor and Jean-Rémy Moët met in 1814, and where Napoleon left his bicorne hat for all to see, along with other mementos. But what really captured my attention was all the wine, still *en tirage* (in riddling racks, not disgorged), from vintages going back in time. Way back.

"What year were you born?" asked my jovial host as I gazed longingly over the bottles.

"1948."

"Let's open one from that year."

First, he gave me a vivid lesson on how he blended Champagne. We tasted a blend with wines from several vintages and vineyards he was working on for Dom Pérignon. In these wines, acid is as important as the fruit; the balance was the magic he sought in a finished wine. We spent an hour making a blend, and I was so absorbed in the process, I almost forgot about 1948. Although I was not totally convinced that I warranted waking up the old wine, he opened it.

I expected a tired but polite wine I could respectfully call interesting, but it was so much more than that—it was memorable. The balance of fruit and acid was still in play, as well as a few bubbles to liven it up. I was overwhelmed by his hospitality. Why did I deserve so much of his time along with this rare wine? I was no one, just a working-class vintner from Napa.

When we parted, I wished I had a Napa wine to offer my thanks. I quickly learned to bring a few cases of wine from home to give as gifts—which I discovered were much appreciated.

Case in point: In 1994, I ran into the winemaker of Domaine Comte Georges de Vogüé (a great Burgundian producer) at a New York tasting. In 1983, following a tasting at his winery, I gave him a bottle of Napa

Zinfandel as a parting gift, thinking it would be a curiosity he might enjoy. A decade later, as he poured his wine from behind a table, he looked up, smiled, and said, "Thanks for the Zinfandel. I really enjoyed it." There is a lesson there. Maybe a few.

On Tor's first full day in Champagne, a Moët winemaker pours him a glass from a just-disgorged bottle of Champagne from Tor's birth-year, 1948.

As I said goodbye to my Moët host, I invited him to Napa, hoping I would get the opportunity to return some of his kindness. I circled back to the tourist center to see what hotel had been arranged. My next appointment was the following evening with Mr. Monmousseau for dinner in the Loire Valley.

My childhood was a world with bohemian parents—my father a play-wright, my mother an artist and stage actress. As a family, we never traveled much outside their bookshelves. Summer trips were spent in a station wagon dragging a camper and never leaving the western United States. My only trip outside the continental United States was Vietnam. There, I served in the hospitals, where accommodations were sparse. Being here, now, was the adventure of my life.

Later that evening, I was directed not to a hotel, but to a stunning château perched on a hill that was part of the original Moët family's Résidence de Trianon. From 1805 to 1817, Jean-Rémy Moët, with the extravagant eye of Jean-Baptiste Isabey, built the Résidence de Trianon. A complex of gardens,

Moët & Chandon, Jardins de L'Orangerie

Where there is no wine, there is no love.

—**EURIPIDES**
GREEK PLAYWRIGHT, 480–406 BCE

buildings, water features, and grounds boasting some fifteen thousand plants in bloom during the summer. More than 1,900 feet (600 meters) of boxwoods lined the pool near the orangery, where I would have lunch the next day amid a room full of celebrities and captains of industry.

My room was part of this architectural wonderland, larger than most apartments. The bathroom had a huge marble bathtub—funny how some things you just never forget. Flower arrangements, views, designer furniture, some historic family pieces, and a chilled bottle of Champagne greeted me for the night.

Recently, I found myself shuffling through photos I took during that stay in Trianon, and they still bring smiles. Me in the marble bathtub with a glass of Champagne, views out my window, and pictures of my dinner host in a formal dining room with his daughter.

That evening, I enjoyed the longest meal I had ever had in my entire young life. It set the bar and became the high-water mark for what I would strive to bring back to Napa. I would always be a fan of Moët and Dom Champagne. Was Napa Valley capable of building such loyalty with this level of hospitality, food, and wine? It was a question I would spend the next twenty years answering.

The evening began with introductions. I believe there were four other couples, our host, his daughter—who was conveniently my age—and myself. Our host sabered a magnum of Champagne, and we were off and running for the next three hours. Seven courses built around both rare still wines and the bubbly wines of Champagne, lively conversations, more wines, more small but impeccable dishes that complemented the wines.

The host's daughter invited me to join her and her friends for some serious mountain climbing near Burgundy, where I would finish my trip. She would teach me how to use ropes and pinions, convinced I would love the sport. I declined but was grateful for her hospitality. I had scheduled full days in Burgundy.

The next day, I was invited to a four-course lunch in the formal orangery where Napoleon—and so many other heads of state since—had been entertained. The view was a reflective 164-foot (50-meter) pool and hundreds of feet of boxwoods—a visual kaleidoscope of colors and textures: earth, sky, and water. The meal was better than that of the evening before, staff generously attentive, guests engaged, all senses heightened. Time stood still in the orangery, a building that had seen so much history, the tone in the room pitch-perfect. I had been invited to a brilliantly choreographed concert that would remain with me forever.

With a long drive from Épernay south to the Loire Valley ahead of me, I left earlier than the others. My evening plan was dinner with one of our importers, a château owner. I was satiated, happy, and not concerned I would get lost. As I said my goodbyes, a waiter opened up a box and offered me what was inside. I had never had a cigar in my life, but I was clearly in an open-minded, freewheeling mood, so I took one of the largest in the box, a Churchill. He cut the cigar for me and gave me the fanciest box of matches I'd ever seen.

As I pulled out of the driveway and spread my maps for the journey, I slowed to look back and take it all in—where I had just been, how much I had enjoyed myself, how all my senses had been heightened. Somehow, I knew it would alter my life in Napa. I would do everything possible to bring this level of hospitality to my wine industry in Napa Valley. The French had centuries of practice, and Napa would just be getting started. But I was convinced we were fast learners.

I lit my big Cuban Montecristo Churchill, rolled down the window, and drove south to the Loire Valley to visit a famous sparkling Chenin Blanc producer we imported. I was inspired. From Loire and its castles and expressive wines, I drove to Bordeaux, Hugh Johnson's maps on my lap, and visited the winemakers at Château Latour, Château Montrose, Château Mouton Rothschild, Château Haut-Brion, and Château d'Yquem. Each winemaker signed a label, and I still have many of them. The winemakers must have thought I was a bit crazy, but they were my rock stars, true celebrities.

After Bordeaux, my Peugeot took me to Beaujolais, then Burgundy, and my first three-star Michelin meal, at Maison Lameloise. The sommelier recommended a Domaine Leroy Musigny from the 1960s, which I can still taste today. Palate etching. I visited Domaine de la Romanée-Conti and met winemaker André Noblet for the first time and took extensive notes on his philosophy of winemaking and growing. Last stop Alsace, a war-ravaged northern area turned into an epicenter for restaurants, small and magical villages, and brilliant white wines.

This adventure lasted almost three weeks. I was paid a salary from beginning to end. Fine wine had brought many of us together, forged friendships and lifelong memories. I was in the right business.

Label signed by Domaine de la Romanée-Conti winemaker André Noblet in 1981, during Tor's first visit to the legendary winery

In Europe then we thought of wine as something as healthy and normal as food and also a great giver of happiness and well-being and delight. Drinking wine was not a snobbism, nor a sign of sophistication, nor a cult; it was as natural as eating and as necessary.

—ERNEST HEMINGWAY
AMERICAN AUTHOR, JOURNALIST, AND SPORTSMAN; 1899–1961;
FROM A MOVEABLE FEAST

MAY

PERSPECTIVE AND PREPARATION ARE KEY. It is time to kick dirt, get out in the vineyards, tie up new contracts, renew the old ones, get a last-chance perspective on where you are going for this vintage. In the vineyards, flowering begins. I can walk my vineyards and see them come alive, preparing for the young grapes to set. This gives us a glimpse of what crop size we might anticipate. Vines, unlike most plants, don't need pollinators—they self-propagate—but good weather is essential. Late frost and heavy rains during flowering can severely limit the crop size. Flowering is a very sensitive time for any plant.

In the winery, it is also the last hurrah to make any changes in the Cabernet blends. By May, the winemaker knows each barrel intimately and should know where each is going before bottling. I believe this is essential—the knowledge of each barrel's strength and where it fits or doesn't. The same wine will taste a little different in each barrel—simple when you remember that the staves of each barrel often come from different trees in the same forest, and sometimes different forests, and are bent and put together by a cooper's hand over a slightly different fire. No two fires are alike, even though barrel coopers strive for uniformity. I'm a firm believer that in the best wineries, the winemaker knows each barrel, rates it, and finds the right home for it. The wine from the barrels that don't make the cut is sold. Breaks my heart when this happens, but it does. The best wine wins, as my team knows well, and can't be compromised.

May is the month to prepare for the summer bottling runs. As I mentioned earlier, bottlings are Murphy's Law personified. Be prepared or die. Make sure you have the exact number of bottles (glass), capsules, labels, special formats (bottles to be hand-etched) ordered and ready to show up on time at the winery. Did you get all the label approvals from the Bureau of Alcohol, Tobacco, Firearms and Explosives (BATF)? Yes, the government must sign off on every aspect of every label. Mistakes in this boring arena are costly. I've made a few, but I like to think I've learned from my mistakes. For the upcoming harvest, the new barrels haven't shown up yet, but it's time to think of racks, space, and bins and start preparing fermentation spreadsheets.

If a winemaker wants to take a little vacation—and I mean a little one— May presents a window.

NAPA VALLEY AND BORDEAUX—A PERSPECTIVE

How can both Bordeaux and Napa Valley make world-class wine from the Cinq Cépages, or Bordeaux, varieties—Cabernet Sauvignon, Merlot, Cabernet Franc, Petit Verdot, and Malbec? They are half a world apart, different latitudes, soils, and climates, and yet they make incredibly similar high-quality wines. I was in both Bordeaux and Napa Valley in August 2018 and was once again reminded how differences can cancel each other out and make these growing areas so alike in the critical areas: the quality of the fruit and the time it is harvested.

Let's take a closer look at how this is possible. It is a fascinating perspective when you lay it all out, and there is always danger when you think you have it all figured out. So, let's have some fun and look closely at the magic that makes greatness possible for world-class growing areas a vast ocean and continent apart. A reminder—water may separate the continents of the world; it is wine that brings them together.

In 2018, I was the tour guide for a group of fellow Americans who wanted to see Bordeaux through my eyes. I had lined up a wonderful representation of châteaux from most of the key appellations on the Left and Right Banks of Bordeaux. We toured the cellars, tasted, kicked the vineyard dirt, and by the time the two weeks were over, many knew enough to be dangerous. I will never forget when we visited Château Margaux, seeing the winemaking team taking vineyard fruit samples on Segways, their heads smoothly gliding along the tops of the vines. That was a first, and my winemaker now wants his own Segway.

I visited Bordeaux often in the eighties as an importer, an insider, and I had an intimate view of how Bordeaux functioned as a growing area and as an immensely successful multibillion-dollar industry. Bordeaux, when you take it all in, is vast, encompassing 287,000 acres in vines. Napa Valley, in comparison, is small, consisting of 46,000 vine acres. Out of the world's wine production, Bordeaux makes 2.6 percent, Napa Valley 0.4 percent—or 4 percent of the wine made in California. Size matters.

Bordeaux on the Left Bank, home to all the First Growths, is relatively flat. Only in the Right Bank do you see more serious visible elevation changes. Napa is surrounded and defined by well-defined mountains with elevations over 2,000 feet (610 meters). Bordeaux is around the latitude 45 degrees north. Napa is at the latitude 38 degrees north. Latitude during the growing season dictates the length of the days in each growing area and the intensity of the sun. Curiously, the accumulated heat indexes from May 15 to August 10 in both growing areas almost catch up to each other and come in with very close relative numbers by harvest.

In the eighties, I wrote research papers for Beringer called *The Vineyard Report*. Doing the research, I discovered there are several influential differences between the two growing areas, one being latitude. The two nearby oceans, the Atlantic and the Pacific, as well as the differences in elevation also influence the vineyards. A closer look at these two factors, and it starts getting very interesting.

Off San Francisco Bay's Golden Gate, in April 1980, when I did this research, the Pacific registered 55.4 degrees Fahrenheit; the Atlantic off the West Bank of Bordeaux was 52.5 degrees. Because of this and the shorter days, Bordeaux would get off to a late start if it was running a race against Napa to ripen grapes. By September, dramatic changes in the warm Gulf Stream off Bordeaux significantly altered this dynamic. The days and the nights are warmer. In July, the waters off Bordeaux are 68 degrees, and in August 68.2 degrees. Bordeaux is catching up fast.

Not so in Napa. In September, as frigid Pacific currents come down from Alaska, the temperatures off San Francisco held to a cold 58 degrees. Warm to hot days and cold nights. Swings between nighttime and daytime temperature in September and October are often fifty degrees. Temperature swings off Bordeaux during these critical months are closer to thirty degrees.

These swings are observed and tracked more closely now than in the eighties, when I did my reports. Records are maintained of the highest temperature and lowest each day—the diurnal shifts, or diurnal swings. Big swings are for those who like good acidity and structure to their wines—acid lover's paradise. Elevation can also play a role in some growing areas where the swings are greater than the valley floors. That is one of the reasons mountain wines (Howell Mountain) in Napa have a slightly different flavor profile than the wines on the floor of Napa Valley.

The important thing with the 1894 Lafite is to taste the wine in its historical context. In 1894, the Impressionists were painting, Brahms was composing, and Paris was just over the Commune.

—MICHAEL BROADBENT
BRITISH WINE WRITER AND AUCTIONEER, 1927–2020

What does all this mean? The cold Napa nights hold the acids, while the warmer daytime temperatures bring rapid photosynthesis and sugars. When harvest suddenly comes to both regions, *kazam*! Bordeaux and Napa are harvested close to the same weeks every year.

The acids and pH of the wines made from the two regions are more similar than many Bordeaux lovers believe. While I worked at Beringer and TOR, I ran comparative lab analysis and knew the data. The two tests I ran on the legendary 1947 Cheval Blanc showed a high-pH, low-acidity, high-alcohol (over 14 percent) wine—more "Californian" than many of the test results I see on some modern Napa Valley wines. But as André Tchelistcheff would say, "It had the flesh," and a good bottle represents a mind-bending experience. It also costs more than many cars on the road today. A note to collectors: the 1948 Cheval Blanc (my birth year) is sneaking up on it. Unfortunately, the few 1948 Napa wines I've had (I still have a few unopened in the cellar) have not stood up to these legends. So few were made, almost none exist.

Add all the statistics up, and in many years, Napa has a greater capacity to reach optimum ripeness when Bordeaux may not. Yes, Napa has more opportunity to explore the riper side of Cabernet if that is the winery style. We have choices and styles, but the best are wines in balance, physiologically ripe, not overripe. Ditto for Bordeaux.

The marine influence also affects rainfall during the growing season. Napa rarely sees rain from May to September. Bordeaux relies on rain, but not too much, during those months. They were spraying for mildew when I visited Bordeaux in 2018; they had a very wet, early season. In Napa, mildew is rare. In 2018, we were dry until a few early light rains in September, which only washed off the dust and freshened things up. It is against the law to irrigate during the growing season in Bordeaux. Not in Napa. In both regions, the secret is to under water but keep the vines alive. Too much water can impact quality in negative ways.

In Saint-Émilion in 2018, I visited a small tourist vineyard with singular rows of all the Cinq Cépages Bordeaux varieties. They were all ripening at different times. Cabernet Sauvignon was weeks ahead of the Petit Verdot. It was fascinating and caught my attention. Out of curiosity, I called my winemaker in Napa that night and asked him how each of these varieties were maturing in most of Napa. He said they were on the exact same timetable as Bordeaux in Oakville, where we have blocks of Cabernet Sauvignon, Petit Verdot, and Cabernet Franc.

In 2018, both Bordeaux and Napa Valley made great wines that were harvested very close to the same dates. I'm relatively sure in several vineyards, separated by a continent and ocean, the exact same dates. Just logical.

The next two stories in this chapter are the grower's stories, on how to look for and plant a vineyard. One tells of how the mountains that surround Napa Valley can affect a vineyard, as does each vineyard's relationship to cool marine influences. It is also a cautionary tale. The other is how the plant material, or clones, can affect the taste and overall character of a wine, and the joys of winemaking. Both stories taught lessons through mistakes and success.

ON PLANTING A VINEYARD

Susan and I planted a small vineyard in front of our new home in the middle of Napa Valley in 2020. It is a great location for a vineyard making exceptional wine, with Spottswoode Winery as a neighbor, but we will never make a profit based on what we paid for the land, at least in our lifetime. Oh, well—it looks great as we drive home. We did the same thing over thirty years ago. Funny, I swore I would never do it again, but here I go—again.

Why do I struggle with this? I love walking vineyards, kicking Napa dirt. However, when you come home from a long day at the winery or walking other growers' vineyards and you drive through your own vineyard, it always begs for attention. Like the sirens of Ulysses, it beckons, "Come, come and make sure all is well, come to me."

When I was younger, thirty years ago, I was lured by this song. I would stop and walk the rows, drop clusters that touched, do a little leafing or suckering. Petting the animals. Now, when I arrive home after a day's work at the winery, it is not what I need. I need a nice glass of wine, a little Coltrane on the turntable, and blissful ignorance of the news, other than what my wife has been up to during her day. I don't need sirens in my vineyard late in the day at my age. I also go to bed earlier than I did thirty years ago. It's a process.

But time heals all or allows us to selectively forget what we want to, and I'm once again planting a small vineyard that I can't get to unless I drive through it. I already hear the sirens huddled among my new Cabernet Franc clone 214 vines calling me: "We are the clones of 214. Come to us."

I don't like the term *clone*; it sounds like something from a *Terminator* movie. I wish we could name the plant material like they name the roses my wife loves and is planting around the vineyard. Roses have colorful names like Braveheart, Julia Child, Lichfield Angel, Star of the Nile, Frida Kahlo, Lord Mountbatten—you get my drift. No, we give our cuttings unexciting names like 337, 214, 4, 6, 7. They come from nurseries, virus-free, clean, ready to go.

Clones. Boring, except perhaps when one ventures into the dark world of suitcase clones. These are the outlaws in the world of wine grape clones. To obtain a suitcase clone, you simply visit a famous vineyard (think Pétrus, Le

Pin, Mouton, and so on), and, with the permission of the owner, take cuttings, put them in your suitcase, fly home, and plant them in your vineyard. Easy—one hundred years ago. Not so much now.

The Transportation Security Administration and the Department of Agriculture do not like you to have these in your suitcase. Owners don't like you going into their vineyards and taking cuttings in the dead of night—or anytime. If you get over these two very large hurdles and plant your mysteriously obtained suitcase clone, it just might have some deadly (for the vines, not us) virus or bug that your neighbors might not appreciate you sharing.

Nearly fifty years of walking Napa Valley, I've come across several virus-laden vineyards planted with suitcase clones. Not all these outlaws are infected with a virus, but many are. Several admired suitcase clones, brought in from Europe over the last two centuries, have been heat treated, or "cleaned up" of viruses in nurseries and given another life, and a number. Many of Napa Valley's most successful clones have traveled this route.

To be honest, I'm infatuated with some of these clones, or cuttings, that originated from a suitcase, taken from a famous vineyard, often someplace in France. I love tasting the wines made from them and listening to the renegades who first planted them. They bend convention to pursue greatness. They are all gamblers, and some like a good bar fight now and then, but there is gold down deep in their hearts. They want to put magic into a bottle and share it with their friends. I have tasted some of this magic, wines that taste like no others, very rare and inspiring for a winemaker, and I've also witnessed disaster.

I planted my first vineyard with some suitcase clones. My partner in crime was David Abreu, a brilliant and highly respected viticulturist and grape farmer. David has been known to push the envelope, and from his vineyards come many of Napa Valley's greatest wines. Period. He's the vine whisperer. Because of his celebrity as a grower, David is a very hard ticket to get if you want to plant a vineyard, but he was my neighbor in the eighties, and we liked talking about wine and grapes, so he took on my very small project—yep, in front of my house.

We were both infatuated with clones and what was planted in Napa Valley's most celebrated and famous vineyards. Clones weren't discussed as much as they are today, but David and I had our favorites. Somehow, and I really don't know how, David was able to get cuttings from four of our favorite Napa Valley Cabernet vineyards in the 1980s. My memory fades when I'm asked what vineyards they were, or exactly what clones they were, or how David got the plant material. Trust me—these vineyards were and still are very famous, though I assume several have been replanted since.

David planted two rows from each of these four vineyards in the front of my house. I watched them grow. Along with David's crew, we nurtured them to health and finally to the third leaf and our first harvest in 1991.

It was a revelation. Each clone behaved differently on almost every level: the canopy and shoot development, cluster weight and berry size—all different. The grape flavors in each clone from each vineyard, all different. Think about it—every vine was Cabernet Sauvignon, but there could have been four grape varieties in the vineyard when we picked in 1991 and made our first wine. I named it Château La Tor's—A Premier Crew, the latter after my friends who helped harvest. To avoid trademark lawyers, I never sold a bottle, but we did have fun trading and drinking lovely wine. I opened several bottles in 2021, a thirty-year-old wine that raised eyebrows and brought praise in Napa and in London.

Cooper helping Dad lug a box of grapes
at the Kenward home vineyard, 1991

IF I DO HAVE A WINE CELLAR, WHEN SHOULD I DRINK THE WINES I'VE COLLECTED?

Picking the right time to remove a wine from your cellar is like sex in some ways. There are a lot of ways to approach the subject. My advice is to make it very personal. Search diligently for your own drinking windows. Getting there is more than half the fun.

We made wine from this vineyard from 1991 through 1996. We picked, took the grapes to a small winery that Beringer let me construct inside its big winery, crushed the grapes, and made and bottled the wine. One year, Dick Grace and Heidi Barrett made the wine from the vineyard. Every year was a revelation, and all the wines show extremely well today—except for one, but that's another story.

All four expressions of the same grape, Cabernet Sauvignon, showed up every year. What also showed up was some virus. Every year, it became more prevalent, and I would have had to replant eventually if we hadn't sold our home and moved. In the new vineyard, no suitcase clones. I loved adventure but wanted a vineyard to stay healthy for the rest of my life. This Cabernet Franc clone 214 is virus-free and from a highly respected and certified nursery. The clone originated from the Loire Valley in France, and Tracey and John Skupny and Russell Bevan, winemakers I respect, gave me a huge thumbs-up after working with this clone for several years.

The sirens call me as I drive through my tiny, young vineyard, but I let them be and work my way to my wine cellar to pick out a bottle for dinner. Maybe a little Coltrane or Getz, Puccini, John Prine, or Lennon-McCartney streaming around me as I pull the cork. My taste in music is like the wine in my cellar—very eclectic, occasionally eccentric, but all with inspiring backstories like the wineries I have visited, winemakers I know, winemakers I would like to meet. They offer a little peace in the storm, and a chance to travel to faraway lands in my living room. I do not venture into the vineyard outside, unless our puppy, LuLu, insists it is playtime.

I personally made these "homemade" wines from my clonal experiment vineyard, Caymus Vineyards (thank you, Chuck Wagner), Bancroft Ranch, State Lane, and Chabot Vineyard over a twenty-year span. One to two barrels a year, very hands-on, a time to experience winemaking on a micro scale, get our hands dirty, share time with friends willing to buy my Tom Sawyer promise of work disguised as fun. Cheap labor, and, in the case of family members, child labor. Wonderful memories and lessons learned.

On the twentieth anniversary of TOR Wines, we opened all the wines (beginning with 1983 and ending with 1995) that I had made with friends from our vineyard and others. All wines were wonderfully fresh, very much alive, with some great wines on a plateau I sense will go on for a while. But drinking windows are very subjective. That said, a great old wine and a great new wine will always inspire the groups you share them with. If the wine is one you made together, it inspires the best of memories, cementing friendships.

KICKING THE DIRT—AND FINDING A VINEYARD

Occasionally, we all run into someone who tries to convince us in annoying ways that they know everything, and I mean everything, there is to know about wine. How it is made, how to choose a great wine, what is a great wine, what isn't a great wine, the greatest wines they have ever tasted—blah blah blah. Boring and annoying. Your opinion doesn't count; they are the expert in the room. They don't listen. They talk. They never change subjects. I hope this is not your neighbor.

Maybe you are fortunate enough never to have met this person. I have, on several occasions, and my collective memory is that this is someone who has been engaged with wine for, usually, an average of six or seven years. Sadly, I think I was this person at one time—maybe thirty or thirty-five years ago. Now, I know less than I did then. I am no longer an expert. I am curious and learning. I listen to what others say about my wine—even closer when they tell me they are not experts.

The learning curve in the making of fine wine is forever. This should give us humility when we make mistakes. Because we will. Hubris can be deadly if you are a winery owner and are taking a calculated gamble, especially one where you've taken all the chips you have and put them on one bet. This is what I did very early at TOR. It almost dramatically changed the narrative of this book for the worst.

THE CASE FOR HUMILITY

A very influential London wine critic and friend, Harry Waugh, was once asked, "When was the last time you mistook an old Bordeaux for a Burgundy?" His quick retort was, "Not since lunch." Humility comes with experience.

When I started TOR Wines in 2000, our model was Burgundy. After walking through every appellation and most of the vineyards in Napa Valley, where I had the opportunity to taste in bottle, I was convinced that part of the secret to the greatest wines from the valley was finding the best blocks in the best vineyards. The amount of wine made from these small pieces of land would give me only one hundred cases of wine—sometimes more, sometimes less. Finding these gems of land was my quest and still is.

Sure, there are great wines from several vineyards' sites (blends), but the best are made in smaller lots from specific blocks before assemblage. The secret sauce would always be selecting the best-performing blocks over time in the best vineyards. You simply can't get around this if you want to be a world-class winery.

In Burgundy, this is what sets the most expensive wines apart from the others. Burgundy's eighty appellation d'origine contrôlée (AOCs) and vineyards are small and numerous. It has been a grower and négociant world for generations. I invite you to look at vineyard maps of Napa Valley (Vinous has the best and most accurate, and they are available through the Vinous website); you will see that it is made up, for the most part, of a lot of growers—most of them small, and less than 20 acres. Look at the map of Burgundy, and you will see the same, but even more fragmented, because many growers can have their own rows in single vineyards.

In Bordeaux, the acreage is mostly owned by the châteaux, old aristocratic families, and in more recent history, corporations. They are mostly larger tracts of land, far less fragmented. The First Growths in Bordeaux are made in the tens of thousands of cases. The greatest wines of Burgundy are mostly in the hundreds from Grand Cru and Premier Cru parcels that are the family jewels of négociants and wineries. Monopoles—vineyards owned or produced by only one producer/grower—are rarer.

The grower/winery relationships in Napa more and more resemble the Burgundy model to me. The primary difference is the leading red grape: Cabernet Sauvignon, not Pinot Noir.

When I started TOR Wines in 2001, I wanted to work with the best blocks in the best vineyards in Napa Valley. I wanted to have blocks of grapes that would be revered with time, like in Burgundy: Domaine Armand Rousseau's Chambertin, Domaine de la Romanée-Conti's Richebourg, or Domaine Comte Georges de Vogüé's Musigny. These are just a few examples of what I consider their family jewels, which help secure the incredible reputations of these wineries. It would be very hard to put a price on the access to these small blocks of land for these wines. So, I went shopping for jewelry.

Today, I consider our blocks in Beckstoffer To Kalon, Vine Hill Ranch Vineyard, Melanson, and Hyde all family jewels. Before we formed alliances with these growers, I opened wines from these vineyard sites, and I walked them, trying to understand their complexity. The hunt was exciting. Early in my career, I earned a degree in viticulture while working full time at Beringer and thought I knew a few things. If I saw a great vineyard, I would certainly know it after twenty-four years of observation.

Well, I was wrong in one case. But I didn't know it until almost a decade later. This story illustrates my point clearly. We never, ever know it all. We need to stay curious and pay close attention to all the details. There will always be too many important lessons in winemaking to occupy one person's lifetime.

Night-picking Beckstoffer To Kalon—grapes arrive at our winery early a.m., cold and ready to "crush."

The vineyard that illustrates my point was a mountain site that had everything. Famous neighbors who were making many of Napa Valley's cult Cabernets surrounded it. The soils were ideal for the greatest wines—rocky, sparse, well-drained. It had a gentle west-facing slope. In my view, it was close to perfect. No, it was perfect. I had to make wine from this vineyard.

But I had some major hurdles to clear. The main one was bidding on a ten-year contract through a well-connected lawyer for a wealthy individual who owned the property. He bought it, paying a fortune at the time, built a mansion on it, and wanted a fortune in return for his grapes surrounding the mansion. It was a ten-year commitment for some of the most expensive grapes in Napa Valley. But I wanted those grapes and was committed to taking the gamble.

The lawyer and owner narrowed down their search to two potential wineries. My competitor was a cult winery in every way. One-hundred-point wines from the start. This winery had the fame (well deserved), fortune, and status to make this vineyard a star, something I did not have at the time. It also had arguably the best viticulture team in Napa Valley. This very experienced team wanted this vineyard badly.

And the winery, this team, won the contract. I was crushed—that's a good word for a disappointed vintner—but moved on and was fortunate to tie up a three-acre block of grapes in Beckstoffer To Kalon from our friend Andy Beckstoffer soon after.

Looking back, it was fun and frightening being in the hunt. We are family-owned, with no silent partners. The other bidder had partners and very deep pockets. My bet on that vineyard meant I had everything riding on that decision. I would have to take on partners to take on other vineyards if for some reason the vineyard did not meet my high expectations. It was a ten-year contract I could not get out of. However, I felt it was important to tie up the best vineyard blocks, and the rest would fall into place. Calculated gamble.

I know. I know. You want to know the name of the vineyard and the winery that tied up the contract for this incredible vineyard site. I'm not telling. But I *can* tell you what happened to the grapes from this vineyard in those first ten years. I learned the inside story eight years later.

One advantage of making wine in Napa Valley is the friendships and alliances we make with other vintners. We often taste each other's wines, compare, ask questions, and formulate the answers. We learn from one another, we share the good stuff, and we don't hold back. Most of us believe the rising tide benefits all of us in our small valley. This is how I found out what happened to the vineyard I lost so early in my quest for the best.

When I attended a barrel tasting at the mystery winery, I asked why I had never seen a vineyard-designated wine from the vineyard we had both fought for. The owner's name had never appeared on any of its wines. It had location, location, location. Soils, west-facing, great Cabernet appellation, neighborhood—it had it all, except for one major flaw we had both overlooked.

Our dream vineyard was perched dead center in a wind tunnel. The cold Pacific Ocean (55 to 59 degrees during the growing season) and San Francisco Bay, as much as any other single factor, make Napa Valley function as a world-class growing area. Soils are important, but without the ideal climate, you do not have great wines. This marine influence moderates the daytime heat and gives us long growing seasons and grapes with fine acids, ripe fruit, and balance. During our growing season, the warm regions of Napa Valley pull all this cool marine air up and into the valley like a siphon. This is one reason we have cool morning fog that eventually burns off as the day heats up. At night and early morning, the fog rolls back in as grapes ripen. It is a beautiful sight.

There are gaps in the Mayacamas Mountains where this marine influence gets funneled into the valley at specific sites with some velocity, especially in the middle to late afternoon, when it is warmest. Wind tunnels are hidden where you least expect them. One was centered on the vineyard I competed for. It had its own microclimate, greatly influenced by a very cool wind coming off the Pacific Ocean miles away. The grapes rarely reached the physiological maturity the winery deserved. Those cool winds made it a significantly cooler site than its favorite neighbors.

All of us missed how this climatic aspect would influence wines made from this vineyard. The wines told us the true story—they never lie. Wind currents are important to a vineyard—to our eye, the invisible part of its terroir, but not to grapes that want to get ripe. Each year, because the wine from the vineyard didn't meet the cut—which for this winery was very high—it was sold to other wineries for pennies on the dollar. I was not smart, but in hindsight, I was very lucky. Luck in any career shouldn't be overrated. It might even be essential.

We learn about wine, winemaking, winegrowing through experience though our mistakes and success. We have one classroom each year to learn our lessons. There will never be enough classes for us to know all of it. That is the exciting and challenging part of what most winemakers face. It is what makes our learning curve, forever. This is why I have no patience for the wine snob whose opinion is narrow, who talks more than listens, and who has less than ten years of being the expert. Not the life of my party.

The Titanic Swim Team, aka the Kenward family,
crushing grapes for "homemades," 1998

Behold the rain, which descends from Heaven upon our vineyards, and which enters into the vine-roots to be changed into wine; a constant proof that God loves us and loves to see us happy.

—BENJAMIN FRANKLIN
AMERICAN AUTHOR, SCIENTIST, AND DIPLOMAT; 1706–1790

JUNE

JUNE, FOR MOST OF MY NAPA VALLEY LIFE, revolved around the Napa Valley Wine Auction. I served on the Founding Committee, and, like many vintners, I clocked hundreds of volunteer hours supporting the auction over the decades. Now, it is changing direction—no longer a live auction that took years of preparation and planning—so the month will take on a different shape. June, however, will always represent a grand time to show off wines and our hospitality, a warm and wonderful time of year to embrace everything Napa Valley.

In our vineyard, we see the vines pass through flowering into a young, green berry set. But in 2011, during auction week, Napa experienced a freak torrential downpour. All the wellies (rubber footwear) disappeared from the hardware stores, and outside the huge auction tent, I found a few very expensive stiletto-heeled shoes stuck in the mud, abandoned by well-dressed women fleeing the sudden deluge. Hearty red wines were the most favored as the chill set in, more so than previous years. Strangely, everyone got into the celebratory mood and seized the moment. It became a very successful auction, raising $7.3 million for important local charities, mostly health care and education.

The vines, however, did not like the storm at all. That year, I lost 90 percent of my crop in Beckstoffer To Kalon. My blocks were flowering that first week in June, and the hard rain annihilated the flowers, so there was little to no fruit set. It was the hardest hit of all my vineyards. I did make wine that year—just less of it. Mother Nature reminds us in many ways that she is in full charge, and we are in the agricultural business first and foremost. Our moments as international social animals can be interrupted at any time by inclement weather, fire, and earthquakes. I have experienced them all in my decades as a vintner. Mother Nature has my full respect.

June is a superb month to focus on the vineyard—in this case, Napa Valley's most controversial and, in many ways, most successful vineyard as far as accolades or 100-point wines. That vineyard is Beckstoffer To Kalon. I'll start with a focus on the man behind the vineyard's success in modern times. The man who has changed the dynamic of all Napa Valley grape growers, Andy Beckstoffer. For contrast, I'll introduce the MacDonald brothers, Graeme and Alex, who know more about To Kalon than anyone I know, even Andy. They live and work in the original footprint of To Kalon in their great-grandparents' vineyard, which bears their last name. We are all friends, Graeme, Alex, Andy, and I, and our lives are entwined around this vineyard first planted in 1868 and named To Kalon in 1886.

To Kalon—Greek for "highest beauty"—named by its first owner/winemaker, H. W. Crabb, now heralded by Beckstoffer and Mondavi. They are the only ones licensed to use the name to designate a wine. More about this later.

I've known Andy Beckstoffer for four decades. Our paths crossed many times as we served on various committees that supported agriculture and politics. Andy is very political and has set up his will so each of the famed historic vineyards he owns and manages is never sold by family members but stays in vines. He is actively forming alliances among growers and residents to protect the Napa Valley Agricultural Preserve.

The Ag Preserve was established in 1968 by a group of vintners who were true visionaries. They knew Napa Valley would be threatened by developers and needed protecting if it was to remain agriculturally grounded. In the sixties, there were discussions of building an international airport in Carneros. The U.S. Army Corps of Engineers saw rapid housing development and suggested turning the Napa River into a concrete one like Los Angeles. Developers were lined up, projects proposed, but somehow, some way, a small group defied them and established a landmark set of zoning laws that encompasses most of Napa County today. This group of visionaries, attacked and threatened by special-interest groups and individuals, nevertheless managed to make the new zoning laws stick.

Since 1968, Napa Valley has changed dramatically. Andy and I have watched most of this change, and we fight battles every year to keep Napa Valley agriculturally centered. My wife, Susan, is another vocal activist fighting battles against winery projects that seem shortsighted—more in the interest of a few, not the majority, and not the future of a sustainable Napa Valley. I'm surrounded by these activists. Never a dull moment with this group when a skirmish is being waged.

"You need a villain," Andy told me bluntly when I told him I was writing this book. "You need a villain!" He was adamant. He was also visibly excited that I had taken this project on, telling an insider's history of the last nearly fifty years, but he had some strong ideas, and the "villain" was one. The more I thought about it, he was right. A face without teeth looks a bit strange and has no bite. So, I will introduce the villain here, and, as in all good stories, this villain may show up later in this book when you least expect it.

Andy, Susan, and I all agree that the villain is simply individuals and groups who put their short-term interests and profits before the common good. Without conscience, they threaten future generations with an erosion of a quality of life I've enjoyed. The making of world-class wines and growing grapes falls behind short-term profit taking. They attack vulnerability for self-interest with lawyers, guns, and money. A nasty spiral to get caught up in, and some writers claim it is too late. We've lost paradise. I disagree. We need to stay vigilant and take on unpopular battles.

In fairness, we will always have a tug-of-war between growth and no growth, housing developments, low-income housing and McMansions, tourism, traffic, winery definitions, the defining of agricultural boundaries, and what rules we need to follow. There are meetings and decisions about these matters taking place today, tomorrow, and the next day someplace in Napa Valley. It is almost impossible to stay vigilant and informed. Some who have been here for generations think we should have little to no restrictions. Tug-of-war with environmentalists can get bloody. Lines are drawn and redrawn as Napa Valley's popularity as a tourist destination gets stronger.

"In the sixties and early seventies, the growers and most wineries hated the tourists and didn't want the sun to set on them," Andy told me once as we were driving to a 49ers football game. It was the last game at Candlestick, evoking lots of memories for both of us. Andy has a lead foot and can scare the hell out of me in heavy traffic, as he did that day. "Now they embrace them. I wish all the cities—Napa, Yountville, Oakville, Calistoga, all of them—would sit at one table together and figure things out. We have too many fractured interests. We have to find a way to protect the goose that laid the golden egg. I wish we could become a UNESCO area like Saint-Émilion, France." The latter thought is intriguing, but would place too many restrictions on the wineries, and collectively they would pass.

Andy was the right person at the right time when he bought his portion of the original To Kalon vineyard in 1993. Beckstoffer To Kalon is his golden egg, and the way Andy has managed the vineyard and the contracts for the fruit with over a dozen producers has made wine-growing history. Because of his 175 times the bottle price ($300 per bottle × 175 equals $52,500 per ton of grapes), he is as controversial as any grower I know in Napa Valley. The growers who have adopted his model in some form adore him. Many of the producers who believe they can no longer afford the grapes don't. Andy has a lot of energy for a man his age—somewhere in the eighties, he'll tell you. Oh, did I mention his lead foot? He drives through life like he drives through rush-hour traffic. Head on. Give him an inch, and he'll take it.

This is a good place to inject a little To Kalon history. It gives context. In 1868, H. W. Crabb bought 240 acres on the west side of what would become Oakville, a small town with an oak in the middle of the road going up Napa Valley—now known as Highway 29. A wealthy entrepreneur, Crabb planted it to grapes. Before he was done planting, he had over four hundred grape varieties on the property. He liked to tinker. He also built one of the largest wineries in Napa County, and by 1880 it was the third largest. Charles Krug and To Kalon battled it out to claim the title of best winery in Napa Valley. Their wines were shipped all over the United States and into western Europe, where they won international awards for their quality.

Crabb died in 1899, and by that time the vineyard had been decimated by phylloxera, the root louse, which Napa Valley would not entirely recover from until the 1970s; it would take that long just to get back to the production levels of the 1880s. Over those years, To Kalon was sold to many buyers in turn and at one time claimed to be the largest cherry ranch in the United States. In 1939, the To Kalon winery burned down, a shadow of its glamour days. Fast-forward to 1993.

It is my belief Andy Beckstoffer prides himself more as an entrepreneur with a degree from Dartmouth's Tuck School of Business and an environmentalist keen on preserving Napa Valley's agricultural prominence than as a grape grower. That said, he is Napa Valley's most famous grape grower and has earned the recognition though hard work and a vision. In his eighties, tall and athletic, with a southern twang he has never lost after decades in the California sun (unlike his brother who still lives in Virginia), Andy is a commanding presence and is very clear on his larger agenda: preserving many of Napa Valley's historic vineyards. To Kalon, Dr. Crane, Las Piedras, Bourn, Missouri Hopper, and Georges de Latour are the most prominent—and expensive—to make wine from. Every wine vineyard designated from those sites must carry the name "Beckstoffer" before the vineyard's recognition. It is part of the contract.

In 1970, Andy moved to the Napa Valley with his family to establish a subsidiary for Heublein Inc. called Vinifera Development Corporation, which was making large investments in the wine industry. As president of the vineyard development company, Andy managed at one time more than 3,000 acres in vines on the North Coast.

Heublein had bought several wineries in the sixties, the two most prominent being Inglenook and Beaulieu. Beaulieu, under the helm of André Tchelistcheff, had made many legendary wines from great vineyard sites André had coveted—one being an 89-acre piece of the original Crabb To Kalon vineyard. These sites were known at the time as BV #1 through #10 (#3 is called Georges III and #4 is To Kalon). André knew the best dirt for grapes in Napa Valley and coined the term "Rutherford dust" (which refers to wines produced within the Rutherford appellation whose distinct flavors are created by the microclimate and soil structure). André was a mentor to Andy, to me, and to hundreds of others who came to the Napa Valley to make wine. We called him Maestro.

In the seventies, the marketing geniuses at Heublein figured out how to run a winery and make the corporation more profitable for the shareholders. Their answer: sell the vineyards. Their reason: the best wines at the time were all called "reserve" and could come from any vineyard in Napa Valley. You didn't need to own an acre to make a reserve. Grapes and vineyards were all the same, like widgets on a production line. A brilliant winemaker could make reserve wines from up to 25 percent grapes purchased anywhere in California, with the remaining 75 percent from anywhere in Napa. In 1974, the Napa Valley average price for grapes was $336 per ton. Outside the valley, it was less than $100 per ton. Ninety-nine percent of all the Cabernet Sauvignon grapes grown in the Napa Valley went into blends. Diamond Creek's vineyard designates were an anomaly.

"A lot of people get the real history wrong about my purchase of To Kalon, or what was BV #4," Andy told me emphatically. "I did not buy it from Heublein, but from Diageo, which owned the vineyard and was selling it in 1993. Robert Mondavi had first rights but turned it down. His marketing plan was not built around single vineyard designates but "Reserve" wines or blends. I had purchased vineyard Georges III from the Connecticut Mutual Life Insurance Company in 1989—again, not from Heublein, as is widely reported. My thinking was more of a Burgundian

Wine of California . . . inimitable fragrance and soft fire . . . and the wine is bottled poetry.

—ROBERT LOUIS STEVENSON
SCOTTISH AUTHOR AND CRITIC, 1850–1894

model, less of a Bordeaux one, which Mondavi shaped his company after. We were going down different paths."

Andy and I agree on the Burgundian model as a better winemaking fit for what is modern Napa Valley. It is a grower's world, as it is in Burgundy. In To Kalon today, several wineries may have their own designated rows within this 89-acre vineyard to make their wines. At TOR, we currently work with seven distinctly different blocks in To Kalon, and in a single vintage, we have made up to four separate wines that carried a Beckstoffer To Kalon designation. This business arrangement between grower and producer does not really exist in Bordeaux, which is built around usually larger tracks of land owned by châteaux and corporations. It does in Burgundy.

"In the 1980s, I felt the need to shift to more unique 'terroir-based' wines,' Andy explains. "We began to purchase historic vineyards in the 1980s and 1990s. The phylloxera replanting in the early 1990s provided the improved vines. In 2000, we were ready to make the shift." Andy also admits it was a huge gamble. He had put all his chips on his bet that single-vineyard Cabernets and blends would emerge as Napa Valley's future.

It was a good bet. Today, Andy sells Beckstoffer To Kalon grapes for $50,000 a ton. Reserve wines he considers "Barbie dolls." Single-vineyard Cabernets are the real thing. Andy does not make wine; he sells grapes. He initially sold his grapes as Beckstoffer To Kalon, which went on the labels of producers who turned them into 100-point wines. He was getting a lot of attention. He knew the value of marketing and clearly saw his 89 acres of the original Crabb property, Beckstoffer To Kalon, as a brand and a vineyard.

Robert Mondavi Winery was sold to Constellation in 2004, and the company embraced To Kalon–designated Cabernets, but it had a very different perspective on To Kalon's boundaries, which they felt extended considerably beyond the original Crabb To Kalon Ranch—of which they owned over 100 acres. As Tim Mondavi claimed, they could make a To Kalon wine from grapes grown on the moon if they wanted; it was strictly a brand, not a vineyard, not a place.

In 2002, the Robert Mondavi Winery sued Schrader Cellars, which purchased grapes from Andy and put To Kalon on its labels. Andy paid the court costs, and when the lawyers closed their arguments, the future of To Kalon was decided: Andy, and the wineries that bought grapes from his 89-acre vineyard, could use that name on their labels. No one else can use the name "To Kalon," except for the Robert Mondavi Winery, and Mondavi could use it liberally; it was not tied to boundaries.

Old Cabernet vine from the MacDonald vineyard, which is part of the original To Kalon

Opus One (a Mondavi/Mouton Rothschild partnership) owns some of the larger blocks in the original 240 acres, but it goes into the Opus One blend with no reference to To Kalon. "To Kalon" adorns the entrance to the Mondavi winery, and the winery tour guides claim it owns over 500 acres of To Kalon, but there are no drawn legal boundaries to "To Kalon." It is complicated. Legally, it is a brand.

Not even neighbors like the MacDonalds, whose small 15-acre vineyard was part of the original Crabb To Kalon vineyard and borders part of Mondavi's and Andy's To Kalon, can use the name. To complete the story of To Kalon, this is a good place to introduce the MacDonald brothers, Graeme and Alex. It has a happy ending, even though you may never see "To Kalon" on one of their labels.

On the western bench just above Beckstoffer's piece, near the Opus blocks, is a special, rocky 15-acre piece of land farmed by Graeme, home to the MacDonald wine brand managed by Alex. Most of the original To Kalon is an alluvial fan of broken rock materials and soil washed into the western bench above Highway 29 in Oakville. Satellite imagery maps show where ancient streams ran though the property. Having walked most of To Kalon many times, I would guess the rockiest part of the original To Kalon is the MacDonalds'. It also has some of the oldest Cabernet vines in Napa Valley, dating back to 1954, the year Graeme and Alex's great-grandparents took over the property.

Alex and Graeme are two of the nicest, most dedicated wine aficionados I know. They are so nice, so perfect for the job they've inherited, it hurts. It's like they came out of a Disney or Hallmark film. Well-mannered, kind, and passionate, they always make me smile when our paths cross—so much good juju in the air. Graeme went to the University of California, Davis for a degree in viticulture and enology. His first job was at Colgin Cellars, and he has since worked for several of the cults, with a track record of making excellent wines. He has dedicated himself to a very serious study of everything To Kalon: its history, the personal letters of Crabb, old maps— no one knows more about To Kalon than Graeme and Alex.

Like Graeme, Alex knows fine wine as well as any of his peers and manages MacDonald's marketing/sales side. He also has a very good golf game, which I know firsthand. In 2004, the MacDonalds began experimenting with making wines from the old vines from the vineyard. Today, they meticulously make about 250 cases a year, every aspect from vine to bottle scrutinized and fine-tuned. Yes, the wines are exceptional, and it's hard to get on their mailing list.

Before the brothers made wine from their vineyard, it all went to Robert

Mondavi and, before that, Charles Krug, when Robert was involved in the family operations. In the fifties, Robert considered the grapes some of the very best the Charles Krug Winery worked with, and they went into the famed Red Stripe bottlings. In 1966, the first vintage for the new Robert Mondavi Winery, all the MacDonald grapes went to Robert. The agreement was a handshake and has remained so. All but Alex and Graeme's 250 cases of valuable old vine juice goes to the Mondavi winery.

I'm fortunate to have many old and historic wines in my home cellar. Several decades ago, I purchased several bottles of the 1965 Krug Red Stripe. It was Robert Mondavi's last wine at Krug and had MacDonald grapes as part of its profile. Every time I opened the wine, I was reminded of how well some wines from Napa Valley age. It remained vibrant, young, and captivating, defying gravity and other laws of physics over the decades.

Matt Deller, MW, who worked for me, invited me to a meeting of Masters of Wine who had made the pilgrimage to Napa Valley. I brought a bottle of the 1965 Krug with me, not knowing if there would be an appropriate time to open it and share it with the MWs. However, at the end of a very long meal and a lot of speeches, one of which I had to deliver, the opportunity

The original To Kalon Winery in Oakville,
which burned down in 1939

came. The word spread fast, and my table was quickly surrounded by curiosity; it was the oldest wine most had ever had from Napa Valley. It was the wine of the night for many, the wine of the trip for others. It is also a reminder of how great vineyards stand the test of time. Great dirt is great dirt and will always be praised above most real estate if it can make world-class wines through the ages. To Kalon was born in 1868, tasted amazing in 1965, and is making wines that are coveted and very expensive to make and buy in 2022. I sense this will be the same in 2122. I hope so.

A friend of mine, Greg Gregory, took a bottle of my 2013 Beckstoffer To Kalon Cabernet Sauvignon to Steven Spurrier, the father of the Paris Wine Tasting. Steven, who sadly passed away in 2021, was a true gentleman and, in a roundabout way, he and his partner Patricia Gallagher put Napa Valley on the international wine map in 1976. We started a correspondence with promises of getting together on his next trip to Napa Valley, which unfortunately never came about. But after sharing my wine with Greg, Steven wrote me the following note, which I will always treasure:

Dear Tor (if I may),
I have been meaning to write to tell you how impressed I was by the superb
TOR Cabernet Sauvignon Beckstoffer To Kalon 2013 that Greg Gregory had

selected for a predinner tasting for his colleagues from the financial world in London last month, to which he was kind enough to invite me.

I had, of course, heard of the To Kalon vineyard and have tasted a few examples, from Mondavi in the past and occasionally it is part of a blend of top Napa Cabernets, but it is a very long time since I have tasted a 100% To Kalon and never from the famous Beckstoffer vineyard. I was asked by Greg to make a few comments to the group and really all I came down to was the wonderful combination of discrete power and elegance and an exceptional vineyard expression. When the great Harry Waugh tasted Chateau Latour 1961, his remark was "lots of colour and bags of fruit." I probably did a little better than that, but when you have a wine like this in your glass, it really doesn't need descriptives.

Many thanks to you and Greg for this memorable moment.

Best regards,
Steven Spurrier

Thinking back, I'm reminded why a wine's first duty is to be shared with friends who honestly appreciate its virtues. Wine fosters long friendships. That has been my experience time and time again.

Salute!

WINE DESCRIPTIONS

We know everyone perceives the flavors in wine differently. The studies are out. Trust me. Your blackberry might be closer to my blueberry, and if you've never tasted a cassis berry, you have no clue what a wine writer is saying when they use cassis as a Cabernet descriptor. I'm not convinced many writers who use it have tasted cassis—but I'm getting off track.

When we read wine descriptions, they get us into a ballpark of flavors, textures, and sensations. Take them as you would a traffic sign: observe, then go ahead and do what you normally would do based on years of driving. If you're lucky enough to have a regular tasting group, have everyone write descriptions for three wines, and put them all in a hat. Next, pull out each description and have everyone (but the author) guess which wine is being described. It's enlightening. Good thing is, no one is wrong. Everyone is right.

*Wine is the pleas-
antest subject in the
world to discuss. All
its associations are
with occasions when
people are at their
best: with relaxation,
contentment, leisurely
meals, and the free
flow of ideas.*

—HUGH JOHNSON
BRITISH WINE WRITER, B. 1939

JULY

IN JULY, I OFTEN GET QUESTIONS about the vintage: "Give us a prediction on the vintage. Good year?" July is *way* too early for anyone but a fortune-teller to do this. That said, we are forming early opinions, and in the back rooms of our tattered minds, hope reigns eternal. Before the month is complete, we see the size of the grape set, and some viticulturalists will make early predictions on the size of the grape crop. My experience is to not take these too seriously. Many early predictions have been way off—2018 and 2005 come to mind. Harvest generally starts 120 days after the fruit is set. The race is on, with many laps ahead. It is a long race—one most often decided in the hundred-meter sprint at the end.

Bottling season is in the rearview mirror before the clock runs out in July, thank goodness, so we can breathe easier. This reminds us that making wine also involves selling wine. We have bills to pay, people to see. It is a great month to get out and spread the word, pull the corks on new wines, dust off and buff up the wine rhetoric, and greet those who support us. It's time to see the wine buyer—they keep the lights on. My belief is that if you don't embrace this critical element of the wine business, you are leaking oil, and we all know what that can do to a smooth-running internal combustion engine. Remember who allows you to keep the winery doors open. Respect their curiosity and encourage their enthusiasm. Don't be the artist who's always on retreat.

I met many friends while I opened bottles I helped make, and I shared stories about making those wines during Julys past. These conversations always veered away from wine. Julia Child talked politics (a subject I now largely refrain from), restaurants, food, and people gossip. Golf, fly-fishing, and family are always good rabbit holes to explore for me.

The harvest will begin for many in August, certainly for all the sparkling wine producers. (Some pick as early as late July.) So, July is *the* month to get out and spread the word, remove corks, share your handiwork, spread the gospel, and meet the gatekeepers and influencers head-on.

NAPA VALLEY'S GREAT AMBASSADORS 1970–1985: ON THE ROAD AGAIN

On a cold December day in 1984, outside Sparks Steak House on Forty-Sixth Street between Second and Third Avenues in New York City, Paul Castellano, kingpin of American organized crime, and Thomas Bilotti, captain of the Gambino crime family, were executed Mafia style. The three gunmen pulled their semis from trench coats, fired accurate headshots, ran, and were never seen again.

Sparks was a regular hangout for members of organized crime, but it was also a favorite of anyone who loved wine and some of the best steaks and biggest lobsters in New York City. I know. I dined at Sparks a few days before this gang war started. Some things, you don't forget.

One of the sweetest guys I have ever met in the wine industry, Pat Cetta, owned and operated Sparks. He called us all "beautiful" and made us feel he meant it. If I was traveling from the West Coast with a Beringer winemaker in tow, Pat would pick us up in his Jeep Cherokee at JFK and personally drive us to the restaurant for dinner. Below us in his cellar lay over 100,000 bottles of wine Pat had curated. A very large portion of that was from Napa Valley. He loved us, our wines, and our entrepreneurial spirit. I think he also loved the underdog. We loved him back.

On my very first trip as a vintner to New York, I brought Beringer winemaker Myron Nightingale with me to show off our wines to the trade and gatekeepers. Along with the usual suspects was Terry Robards of the *New York Times*. It was 1980. Sparks was on the agenda. New York was a very hard nut for a Napa Valley vintner to crack in those days. A strong base for Western European wines, weak for California. Frankly, California's wine reputation was more about Central Valley jug wine, less about world-class Cabernet Sauvignon. This began to change rapidly in the late eighties and nineties, but in the seventies and early eighties, Napa Valley had a small East Coast profile. We were the underdogs. However, we had some extraordinary champions dedicated to changing our image, and Pat was one.

In the late seventies, Gerald Asher, a wine writer for *Gourmet* and a wine importer, and Paul Kovi and Tom Margittai of the famous Four Seasons Restaurant (epicenter of the New York power lunch), dreamed up an annual event to profile California wines. They named it the California Vintners' Barrel Tasting. It was not really a "tasting" but a four-hour bacchanal that quickly became legend and a highly anticipated annual event at the Four Seasons restaurant.

By the early eighties, it was the most anticipated New York city wine experience and event of the year. Nothing compared to it. The *New York Times* reported that the 1981 tasting and dinner had 2,542 names on the waiting list: 224 filled the room—73 were news media, 111 other restaurateurs. I had a very hard time getting a ticket in 1981, and it blew my mind.

That year, the dinner consisted of eleven courses with twenty-nine California wines poured into six thousand glasses throughout the four-hour show. Six-hundred-twenty-four bottles of wine were consumed, along with ten cases of mineral water. Eleven hundred frog's legs, thirty rabbits, twenty-five goats, seventy-five ducks, and countless oysters were served that night, chopped and sliced into elaborate dishes. The uniformed staff, in dazzling military precision, moved all that in and out of the huge pool room without a single incident.

To this day, I have yet to see a restaurant spectacle to match this one. It is incredible in retrospect that all this was designed to bring attention to California wines. In the event's early years, it was not easy finding enough California wineries to show up in New York and endure this revelry. They had to dig. The night I attended, one shy vintner introduced his wine by saying—maybe half-joking, maybe not—"I'd rather be on my tractor."

After a decade, the organizers burned out and retired the show. With the help of wine and food writer Anthony Dias Blue, a few of us vintners tried to resurrect this show at the 21 Club, the Rainbow Room, and the Pierre hotel, but it was never the same. The Four Seasons California Vintners' Barrel Tasting had the magic we could not duplicate. Most important, though, it let the East Coast know we were not going away—we were just getting started.

WHAT SHAPE OF WINEGLASS SHOULD I USE?

Twenty-five years ago, Claus Riedel designed the perfect wineglass for me while I was at Beringer. We both thought it perfect for the wines it was designed for. It now looks like a lot of other glasses I see. After all these years, I still experiment, and I believe there is no perfect wine glass. I'm more fascinated by how it feels in my hand, how it swirls a wine, and how the wine smells afterward. There are so many great wineglasses today. Experiment, but all the best curve inward toward the top and fit your nose very nicely.

Pat Cetta shared the enthusiasm, and his extensive California wine list was proof. When Myron and I arrived at the restaurant for our first visit, Pat greeted and escorted us to a table set for three. He never left the table until we finished our meal, and he opened over a half dozen bottles of wine in addition to the ones we brought to show off. We tried most of the sides from the menu, including a memorable creamed spinach.

Myron Nightingale started (as he would always do, if given the opportunity) with a Beefeater martini, followed by a rare New York strip. I stayed with wine and had my very first lobster. Sparks was equipped with a tank of live Maine lobsters, and on the menu, it boasted they were "twelve-pounders." Being young, naive, and indestructible, I ordered one. I almost finished it. Almost. The image of Pat and Myron giggling under their napkins at my efforts is indelible. I have never ordered a lobster over four pounds since that evening.

Pat died in 2000, breaking many hearts—blue bloods; mobsters; and steak, lobster, and wine lovers who enjoyed his warm and genial hospitality. He welcomed us all as *famiglia*. He, and the organizers of the Four Seasons Big Show, had given us Napa Valley vintners hope that our wines had champions in the tough New York/East Coast market. With their help, we got our foot in the door. We salute you.

Another group of trailblazers in the early eighties was an assembly of Napa Valley vintners who called themselves the Flying Circus. It began with two or three Napa Valley wineries using the Domaine Chandon jet and chef, then expanded and traveled commercially over a five-year span to all major US metropolitan wine markets. I joined the Circus in 1983.

While I was searching files to put this book together, I found a small clipping from Philadelphia's *Observer* titled "Napa Valley on Tour." The dateline was February 18, 1985. In a photo in this clipping, I see eight individuals in our Circus from that year. One ringleader was Jack Cakebread, on the left. Next is Pam Hunter, our PR person, who put together our agendas, tastings, lunches, seminars, and dinners. Next to her is Bernard Portet, founder of Clos du Val. Bernard, being a French vintner and waving the Napa Valley flag, was a powerful weapon in our battle for attention. He grew up on the estate of Château Lafite Rothschild, where his father was the general director. Charming, dedicated man.

In the photo, I'm in the middle of this motley crew—my role was moderator. Next to me towers Stu Smith (Smith-Madrone Vineyards), a champion of the small guy. Next to Stu is Marcia Mondavi, who has seen more Napa Valley history than any of us. John Wright, from Domaine Chandon, who along with Jack Cakebread was one of the ringleaders, is on Marcia's shoulder. Next to him is my buddy and partner in crime at

Napa Valley On Tour

Six Napa Valley vintners poured a selection of 12 premium wines when they hosted a benefit tasting for the local chapter of the American Cancer Society in Philadelphia last November. The benefit was one of three during a fall tour, which also included Atlanta and Denver. The group travels together twice yearly raising money for community charities and promoting Napa Valley wines. Chef Philippe Jeanty of Domaine Chandon was flown in to prepare a pess luncheon at the home of Norman and Suzanne Cohn during their Philadelphia visit. Pictured above in the Cohn's home are Jack Cakebread, Cakebread Cellars; Pam Hunter, the group's publicity director; Bernard Portet, Clos du Val; Tor Kenward, Beringer Vineyards; Stuart Smith, Smith-Madrone Vineyards; Marcia Mondavi, Robert Mondavi Winery; John Wright, Domaine Chandon; and Ed-Sbragia, Beringer Vineyards.

News clipping from the Observer *in Philadelphia, of the Napa Valley's Flying Circus—early ambassadors*

Beringer, winemaker Ed Sbragia. Ed had taken over the head winemaking position from Myron, who retired emeritus.

In every city, we put in twelve-hour days—seminars, and long, elaborate lunches and dinners, lots of wine, and lots of speeches. Together, we told the Napa Valley story, and we worked well as a team. We enjoyed traveling together, found time for some practical jokes. We left one vintner, who didn't answer our calls in the early morning because he was still on the town, behind. Somehow, he found us by lunchtime in another city that same day. He struggled through dinner, but we covered. Name withheld.

Several decades later, Jack Cakebread invited the living members of the Flying Circus for lunch at his winery. It was after Napa Valley had survived a devastating fire in 2017, and the 2014 earthquake was still on our minds. He wanted to relaunch the Circus, or maybe he just wanted to see us all together again—revive some of the days from the Wild West.

Or maybe he wanted to be reminded of what a strong community we can be when there are big challenges in front of us. Together, we've survived recessions, earthquakes, and fires in the years since I had moved to Napa Valley. Jack has seen us band together to get through the worst of times and work together. He tells a story about his tractor breaking down at a critical time in his early years and Robert Mondavi loaning Jack one of his. Robert often talked about the importance of supporting the new vintners in the valley. They were needed to spread the word, rise the tide, and make world-class wines that caught the attention of the wine trade, the consumers, and the gatekeepers.

THE GATEKEEPERS

In the seventies and early eighties, wine writers who influenced the fine-wine market, moving dozens or hundreds of cases with a single endorsement, could be counted on one hand. Many had presence, but few significantly moved wine. That would change quickly and dramatically.

It was a white-male-dominated group with some exceptions in the sixties and for the most part in the seventies. Of course, there are some dramatic exceptions. Jancis Robinson began her wine-writing career in 1975 and, over many prolific decades of writing, according to *Decanter* magazine, is "the most respected wine critic and journalist in the world." I second this. Karen MacNeil began a wine column for *Elle* in the seventies, then later wrote *The Wine Bible*. Her book is now in its second printing and is the top-selling wine book in the United States. I see Karen often, and she continues to stay amazingly busy with tastings, newsletters, multimedia projects, and updating the *Bible*.

Each time we are in London, Susan and I plan a visit with Jancis and her husband, Nick, to play catch-up. Jancis writes regularly for the *Financial Times*, and her work on two tomes, *The Oxford Companion to Wine* and *The World Atlas of Wine*, has made her an icon in the United Kingdom and the

HOW DO I BECOME A WINE CONNOISSEUR?
Open a lot of wines, then read all you can about them. No short-cuts. Having a tasting group makes it a bit more economical. Make a friend where you like to buy wine, and tell him or her what you like, and see where they take you. A friend will listen to you and not dictate their agenda. Oh, yes—make it fun, and never call yourself a connoisseur.

PS: If you are ripping a lot of corks on the pathway to wisdom, learn to spit. Alcohol is involved and deserves respect.

United States. They are the true reference guides for professionals and laypeople alike. The queen of England listens to her wine advice. Both Jancis and Karen have blogs and newsletters I highly recommend following.

Over the last thirty years, the woman's voice in wine has flourished, and it's as important and vital to the wine business now as that of their male counterparts. Diversity is still an issue the industry grapples with, but there are leaders like Dorothy Gaiter who shine the light for more to enter and find success in wine writing and communications. Let me add that all those who have made their voices heard as successful wine writers over a passage of time have done so through a lot of hard work: Sixty-plus-hour workweeks are the norm. If you want a respected, listened-to voice in wine, you have to work your butt off. I know this firsthand.

The wine books Hugh Johnson (alone and with Jancis), Michael Broadbent, and Harry Waugh wrote were my guidebooks in the seventies, and I used them as constant references in the early eighties, when I worked on my newsletters, the *Beringer Vineyard Report*, and traveled. Robert Finigan had a newsletter on California wines in the seventies; later came the *California Grapevine* and the *Connoisseurs' Guide to California Wines*. With time, many others would cover California wine regularly in the food section of most of the major dailies and magazines.

Wine Spectator began in San Diego in 1976, and I visited the young group of editors in 1978 and contributed a few stories I had written and photographs. They were surviving on a dream. In 1979, successful businessman Marvin Shanken rescued *Wine Spectator* and over the following decades, reshaped it and built it into one of most influential consumer voices in the wine industry. I attended *Wine Spectator*'s first thirty annual Wine Experience events (mostly in New York) as a representative of Beringer and then TOR. The three-day full assault on wine education, tastings, and networking attracts thousands of wine lovers and hundreds of trade people. At one event, I joined Jim Laube, who moderated a panel on the To Kalon Vineyard. We conversed in a room of two thousand people, having donated five cases so everyone could have a small taste of each one of our wines. When Domaine de la Romanée-Conti hosted a panel, they poured many twelve-bottle cases of their prized Pinot Noirs and five of their lovely unicorn, Le Montrachet, which can sell in excess of $8,000 a bottle today.

I fondly remember one of the first *Wine Spectator* Wine Experience events, held at the Fairmont Hotel in San Francisco, before Marvin and his team took full charge. Hugh Johnson talked about Port, "a port in any storm." Later, Robert Parker introduced the lesser-known wines from the Rhône

Valley. The latter made a huge impression on me, guiding me to my love of Grenache and Syrah. It would be the last time Parker and Marvin would share the spotlight together. Parker went on to start the *Wine Advocate*.

James Laube joined *Wine Spectator* full-time in 1983, and along with Parker became a very powerful and influential critic. If he scored a wine in the high 90s, it vanished. Jim had covered several beats for the *Vallejo Times-Herald*; he had even covered the Zodiac Killer case before joining *Wine Spectator*. He was passionate about wine and an excellent writer who rarely needed editing—perfect for the job. As the number of wines tasted grew exponentially, he needed to be efficient and hardworking to keep up

To Kalon panel for the Wine Spectator*'s* New York Wine Experience: *(left to right) Mark Carter, Paul Hobbs, moderator Jim Laube, Tor, and Fred Schrader*

on all the changes. All the wines he tasted and scored, he tasted blind. The *Wine Spectator* business model was subscription and advertising based.

Over the decades, Jim covered in particular California Cabernet Sauvignon and Chardonnay, and he often scored wines from key *Wine Spectator* advertisers poorly, which was not easy on Marvin, but Marvin and Jim were almost like father and son outside the office. They have respect for each other and worked together as a team through *Wine Spectator*'s glory years. Like Parker, Laube had many who attacked him, especially producers who didn't like the scores he gave them. I think Jim took many insults and criticisms personally, but that did not change his MO. Despite rumors, he always tasted blind, called it as he saw it, and remained true to himself as a critic. His books on California Cabernet Sauvignon are reference books for me, especially with the tasting notes on early vintages.

In the late seventies and early eighties, both Marvin Shanken and Robert Parker built very separate empires and would be the dominant gatekeepers, the most powerful influencers by a good margin, for the next three decades. Their endorsement moved wine in significant ways. I watched this from a close perspective. Although they had different platforms, from the onset, they both made huge contributions to wine education and the wine market and sales in general.

The United States is not, and never has been, a wine-drinking nation. We lag severely behind western Europe and most First World countries. We have puritanical roots that go deep. Marvin and Robert took wine to the American masses, made it entertaining, less mysterious, more accessible, and sometimes fun. They became competitors, not friends, and they changed the world of fine wine in big ways, with very different business models. They could make a winery, and many argued they could break a winery. As Beringer's vice president of fun, I was the point liaison with all the wine critics and media. I had a front-row seat while these empires were built and ruled the world of wine.

I second Kevin Zraly's opinion of Robert Parker. Zraly, one of the world's most celebrated wine educators, said in his new edition of *Windows on the World Complete Wine Course*, ". . . a critic named Robert M. Parker Jr. helped demystify the wine-buying experience for the consumer. The founder of the *Wine Advocate*, Parker has a photographic memory, and is, in my opinion, the best wine taster in the world."

Over the years I've known Bob, we've probably tasted together over a thousand wines. My observation is that he is a savant when it comes to this world of wine tasting, memory, and focus. One year, we sat down at Beringer mid-morning and tasted 127 wines from various Beringer Wine estate producers. I listened to Bob—his take on the wines, his likes and dislikes—and took some notes. After fifty wines, my notes went into a shorthand that I had difficulty reading afterward. Bob's shorthand translated into detailed notes on all the wines a few months later in his *Wine Advocate* coverage of Napa Valley that year. I was not surprised. I saw him do this time and time again.

And he enjoyed himself through the 127 wines. He told jokes, some a bit off-color, and we had a great time with the winemakers whose wines we were tasting. Candidly, I truly looked forward to these annual tastings with Bob, for several reasons. His true interest in us and our wines was infectious, entertaining to a degree, and very insightful. I learned more about the wines I was tasting, wine I knew, through his palate. We were both Neil Young fans and listened to Neil and other artists and exchanged notes, but we always came back to the wines and how they were made. He memorized it all. Savant.

One year, he complimented me on one of our early TOR Chardonnays and asked me the price. I responded, and he quickly reached for his wallet, pulled out enough cash for a twelve-bottle case, and put it on the table. "Can you send me a case when you bottle it?" A bit stunned, I of course said, "Yes." "In magnums?" "Yes." Then we went back to business. This is a passionate wine critic who knew what he liked and put his money and reputation on the line.

We had many memorable meals together. The first was with Madeleine Kamman, a chef hired by Beringer and one of my fellow cofounders of the School for American Chefs at Beringer. She was a very opinionated and direct

One not only drinks wine, one smells it, observes it, tastes it, sips it and—one talks about it.

—EDWARD VII
KING OF THE UNITED KINGDOM OF GREAT BRITAIN, IRELAND, AND BRITISH DOMINIONS, 1841–1910

woman, and Bob loved that. He functioned best when people around him gave him their frank opinions of him, wine, and food. He was, in his heart of hearts, a full-blown, full-time consumer advocate. That is why I could never pay for a single meal in his presence. He never compromised his position, never took a dollar from those who made the wine he would judge. No compromise.

We shared other memorable meals—at the Duck House in Washington, DC, the Oregon Grille in Baltimore, the French Laundry in Yountville, and more. On the way to the Duck House, Bob planted a whoopee cushion under my seat. We told bad jokes, ate and drank well, and shared our passion for the wine business. At a Neil Young concert, we were invited backstage to meet the rocker, but Neil never came out. It broke Bob's heart—he loved Neil and his singular rock-and-roll voice, sound, and politics. We never forgave Neil, and after that, we played other rockers when we tasted.

The first time I met and tasted with Bob was at the Four Seasons, in Georgetown, DC. I was with Myron Nightingale, Beringer's winemaker. Bob was developing a reputation as a wine writer, though his day job was as a lawyer. At the end of the tasting, he gave both Myron and me a very early edition, maybe the first one, of the *Wine Advocate*. "Please give me your honest opinion of this," he asked. "I'm seriously considering giving up law and doing this full time. My wife thinks I'm crazy, so please give me an honest opinion. No advertising. Subscription only."

I read it on the plane home. My response to Bob was simply, "Go for it." None of us, certainly not me, had any idea of the power and outreach the *Wine Advocate* would have over the next forty years. It grew from a few hundred of his East Coast friends to the world and 500,000 paid subscribers. When each issue came out, shock waves were felt in every corner of the wine industry. If you weren't a part of this, it is hard to understand just how powerful these seismic events were at the time.

My encouragement came only because his passion for wine was straight-forward and so visceral. Few wine critics have been able to describe a wine in a way you can smell it, taste it, and know it intimately—off the page. He also talked passionately about the winemakers and producers he got to know over his years as a critic. This side of his success is often overlooked. He was and is an immensely gifted communicator.

Bob was also very prolific. Besides the bimonthly edition covering all the major winegrowing regions of the world, the travel, the tastings, he wrote fourteen major wine books, widely considered reference tomes on wine-growing regions and their producers. All were best sellers, and all were translated in over nine countries. Then, important international honors were bestowed. Two French presidents awarded him the country's highest honors, as did Italy's president and Spain's. No other wine writer or critic has shared as many of these stages, or probably will in the future.

Bob was so rightfully proud of the French Chevalier de l'Ordre National de la Légion d'Honneur award, he closed down Daniel's in New York for lunch on August 27, 1999, and he and his wife, Pat, invited many of their friends for a long, wonderful six-course lunch. Of course, no one could pay. I was there, and we all toasted the man and congratulated his team, whom he introduced. It is good to be king. But often, and in Bob's case, his prominence opened him up to criticism and some mean and visceral attacks. *Parkerization* is a word all of us in the wine industry know well. It refers to when producers make wines for Bob's palate, shifting the universal wine paradigm over time to riper, more alcoholic wines. If you read a good deal of criticism about him, you might find a disconnect in this argument. He favors a wine with what André Tchelistcheff called "flesh," but he champions many that are restrained and beautifully balanced.

Parker's early call on the 1982 Bordeaux vintage proved him right (and several prominent wine critics wrong), because the wine had generosity and staying power. He called the vintage his way and went against convention. It cemented his career, as did his popularizing the 100-point scale to evaluate wine.

I once told Bob I did not like some riper Australian wines he was a big fan of, and he smiled and said, "My wife says the same thing to me." And that was the end of the conversation. He called it as he tasted it and stayed true to his palate. I've read some critics who, eager to be part of a certain peer group, seem concerned about their image and the wines they think they should like. This often leads to scores that are all over the place and don't reflect a clear vision. I gravitate toward critics I can count on for consistency and honesty in their interpretation of a wine. Both Laube and Parker had this, like it or not, and if you felt differently, you could navigate the waters safely.

Robert Parker is a phenom, and I honestly don't think any one critic will ever have his defining power over the marketplace again. Certainly not in my lifetime. To my mind, he used his power well and made wine a lot of friends all over the world. I've heard arguments to the contrary, but being an insider, from my vantage point, I disagree. I also find it strange that France, Italy, and Spain have acknowledged his contributions, and the United States has not. When I asked Robert to write the foreword to this book, he said yes immediately. He had not read this chapter or any part of the book. He only wanted to tell it again, as he saw it.

For those who claim that Parkerization or other critics ruined wine, please remember that consumers go where they want and over time will have

Robert Parker receiving the Chevalier de l'Ordre National de la Légion d'Honneur from France's President Jacques Chirac in 1999

the final say on what style or what wines survive or become a collector's commodity. History repeats itself. Time and time again. (Homage to Yogi B.) The styles of wine and food will come and go. So, lighten up, critics of critics. It is about the consumer, the wine drinker, the wine lover, not us. We all perceive greatness or the mundane differently, so give us room to explore.

Today, we have many voices in wine and many ways they communicate. I started with telexes, then landlines, then cell phones the size of bricks, then computers, then the world of influencers, bloggers, SOMM TV, movies like *Sideways*, and other social and media phenomena. I'm a bit of a dinosaur, and not an early adopter to many of these changes.

Sometimes, wine and food criticism seem much more about the reviewer than the wine or the restaurant being reviewed. Sometimes, it is more about attacking another opinion than the wine or producer who made it. Maybe that is part of a political mindset that has seeped into our collective behavior. I hope not. For a vintner, optimism is essential to survival. You're dealing with Mother Nature, and she can be fickle, cruel, and wonderful. Water separates the continents. Wine brings people together. I can't find the person responsible for this concept or quote. Maybe it came out of the ether. *In vino veritas.*

Never did a great man hate a good wine.

—FRANÇOIS RABELAIS
FRENCH WRITER, c. 1494–1553

AUGUST

EVERY PLANT BEARING FRUIT in Napa Valley is alive and strutting its stuff in August. Tomatoes are coming in and filling the kitchens—fruit of all kinds. Zucchini can be so prolific and pervasive, you find yourself saying "No, thank you" to the neighbor bearing a basket of them at your front door. This is the only time of year that we lock our front door—to avoid the bags of zucchini friends and neighbors try to pawn off on us. The restaurant chefs are enjoying this cornucopia of ingredients that are fresh and in season. Some of the white wines, like Sauvignon Blanc, trickle in, and the sparkling wine producers are winding it up or are done. The days are now getting shorter but warmer.

Veraison (when the green grapes turn color) begins. This is critical on many levels. For one, it is your last chance to remove (thin) clusters that are not ripening evenly or simply to reduce a large crop to a more balanced one for the vineyard. Managing balance in the vineyard is a true art and needs an experienced eye. I believe that the best and most consistent producers have the experienced eyes when determining crop balance each year. This can take decades of observation. Getting it right can make the difference between a good wine and a great wine. Fruit can be thinned after veraison is complete, but I prefer before. Once veraison is over and the colors are set, harvest is generally forty-five days away for most of the red wines and bolder whites.

August is my last chance to throw big dinner parties and be social with family and friends until Thanksgiving. September, we'll see Chardonnay come in, and September and October, we'll see Cabernet. Harvest moves around some years, but this is what we anticipate. Mother Nature is completely in charge. We just hope she doesn't give us any hard reminders—like long heat waves, early lightning strikes, or fires.

NAPA VALLEY AND THE CULINARY REVOLUTION: THE MID-EIGHTIES TO TODAY

Julia Child brought the sumptuousness and glory of French cooking into our living rooms through television and into our kitchens with her books. She lit the spark of the Culinary Revolution in the seventies, which arrived in Napa Valley in the eighties, then took the nineties with a vengeance. By the turn of the century, Napa Valley was on every foodie's list of places to go and camp. Thomas Keller, the most well-known and decorated American chef of our time, came and set up a permanent restaurant in 1992, but there were legions who built destination restaurants once the revolution arrived. If food and wine have dictated your travel in the last twenty-five years, you've been to Napa Valley.

This is not the Napa Valley I first visited and moved to in the mid-seventies. There were no restaurants, hotels with a star or an asterisk, or even stoplights in Napa Valley. Then, someone flipped the switch, and everything changed. It seemed to happen almost overnight, perhaps because I was so closely caught up in this huge wave that was making its way to the mainland.

Being a small part of the Culinary Revolution in the eighties was like riding a tsunami on a surfboard. You had to pay attention. Time seemed to stand still, almost like a freeze-frame, as it does when your body senses there is a life-threatening or life-changing event ahead. I remember moments like this in Vietnam and once in a near-death auto accident. All your senses are on full alert. Slow-mo. Then, all of a sudden, it's over, and you realize it was a flash in time.

To chronicle this revolution properly requires some great books. I would recommend Joyce Goldstein's *Inside the California Food Revolution: Thirty Years That Changed Our Culinary Consciousness* for good insight into all the players, skirmishes, and joys. And Andrew Friedman's *Chefs, Drugs and Rock & Roll* if you really want to dive into the rabbit holes of the Culinary Revolution in the seventies and eighties. Once you dive in, you may never return to the sunlight the same.

For this chapter, let's follow Julia Child and Madeleine Kamman through personal observations during the late seventies and eighties. I worked and spent much time with both of these women who shaped the culinary world in very different ways. There were grand successes in both their lives—they affected the lives of others, especially those who loved to cook—and there were heartbreaks and failures. Both their careers and lives were influenced by the latter and were inspired by the former.

Julia effortlessly drew us into her orbit. In so many ways, the events that shaped the revolution were like orbiting planets, and Julia was the sun. This physics, I felt, was never her intent, but that's the way it worked. Strangely, after the TV shows had ended, the books she wanted to find homes for set in motion another revolution. From the mid-seventies until she passed in 2004, she cared about placing extensive culinary libraries where they could be shared and enjoyed by broad audiences. Ultimately, she helped establish these libraries at three universities, but it was the University of California, Santa Barbara (UCSB) that ignited some of the first sparks of the revolution, and it was all about finding a home for books.

Julia grew up in a wealthy, very conservative Pasadena family that summered in Santa Barbara during her childhood. She harbored fond memories of the seaside town, whose foremost industry might be tourism. In the seventies, it was the place to be "for the newly wed or the nearly dead," according to the locals. There was the UCSB culture and Isla Vista, just north of town, where students would fall in love with the surfing and the low-key lifestyle and never leave. Santa Barbara in the seventies was where time stopped, until Julia arrived to spend time, reliving the past and quietly shaping the future.

Santa Barbara, of course, embraced her and followed her wherever she would go, taking notes. Hole-in-the-wall Mexican restaurants she visited became shrines. Dinner parties with Julia were the social epicenter of the town, especially with the academia of UCSB. At these parties, the president of the university, board members, and Julia formed a vision: UCSB would house an incredible culinary library she would assemble. Around this comprehensive culinary collection of books, the university would create a school for gastronomy. This was 1979, and Julia and the university president assembled a team of advisers: James Beard, Robert Mondavi, Jeremiah Tower, Alice Waters, and Barbara Kafka.

The Santa Barbara meetings (and some at her home in Cambridge, Massachusetts) started to heat up in the eighties, and I was invited to join the founding board of the newly formed American Institute of Wine & Food (AIWF). I had created several culinary scholarship programs at Beringer, and I was a firm believer that wine should be promoted with food at the dinner table, not as a solo beverage. Beringer stood behind my vision. I did enjoy those meetings in Santa Barbara with Julia and friends; movie stars and great chefs assembled to define their view of the future of American cuisine. Vintner Dick Graff of Chalone became the institute's first president. The foodie tsunami was quietly forming off the coast of sleepy Santa Barbara.

A defining event occurred on May 4, 1983, the date that can be considered the birthday of the Culinary Revolution. I was there, as were four hundred other lucky foodies, chefs, families of chefs, and winemakers. I really don't know who is to blame for gathering us all together. Obviously, Julia had her hand in it, and restaurateur Michael McCarty and chef Jonathan Waxman also take some of the responsibility. One other, often forgotten and not credited, is the general manager of the Stanford Court at the time, Jim Nassikas, who was a brilliant hotelier and a true gourmet who saw a great opportunity and seized it, helped shape it, and truly made it possible in his hotel kitchens and grand room.

An event called An American Celebration was created to draw attention to the AIWF and, most important, the emergence of American cuisine—not French or Italian or that of other ethnicities, but one we could collectively call American. It would be experimental—a melting pot, like American culture—and would reflect fresh, in-season, local ingredients.

This inaugural dinner consisted of eight courses prepared by eight American chefs from all over the United States. For the brave, they added two after-dinner courses by two more famous American chefs and more wine. I presented a Beringer Chardonnay, paired with blackened redfish created by New Orleans chef Paul Prudhomme, almost at the midpoint of the evening.

Paul's dish was surrounded by memorable dishes from Larry Forgione from the River Café in Brooklyn; Jonathan Waxman from Michael's in Santa Monica; Alice Waters of Chez Panisse in Berkeley (a simple fresh garden salad); Mark Miller from the Fourth Street Grill, also in Berkeley (before opening the celebrated Coyote Cafe in Santa Fe); Bradley Ogden from Kansas on his first trip to California; Jimmy Schmidt from Detroit; Jeremiah Tower, also from the Bay Area (pre-Stars/post–Chez Panisse); Wolfgang Puck from Los Angeles (early Spago days); and Barbara Kafka from New York. Maybe, because we were so stunned to have all this talent showing off in one room, we were not overly critical, but my notes on every dish were raves and expressions of awe. Some ingredients, like fiddlehead ferns and cattail sprouts (thanks, Brad), I never knew existed.

I supported the AIWF, with Beringer's investment in this decision, from that night on for the next ten years. (My max for a voluntary board.) Over the next thirty years, I would cross paths many times with all the chefs involved in that dinner, some more than others. Jeremiah Tower and a few friends joined me for lunch at Beringer. We discussed the day he answered an ad in the *San Francisco Chronicle* for a restaurant job in Berkeley. His family had cut him off, and he had just enough coin for the toll returning across the Bay Bridge. He needed the job.

That restaurant was Chez Panisse. Alice Waters interviewed Jeremiah, took him back into the kitchen and had him taste a soup, saying it needed fixing—did he have an idea? Jeremiah tasted the soup and asked if she had a good bottle of wine. She did, and it went into the soup. Jeremiah got the job. In many ways, he helped put Chez Panisse on the foodie trail during its formative years. My other favorite Tower–Chez Panisse story involved a forager who brought in a basket of fresh morels directly from the field. It was Jeremiah's first experience with morels, and he chose to treat them as he did all mushrooms—with a little sauté to kick things off. Within a minute, the walls around the stove were covered with insects that had exited the morels. "I learned quickly that morels are high-rises for insects," he stated. He treated them—and the insects—with more respect in the future.

I visited Paul Prudhomme in New Orleans with friend and writer Harvey Steiman several years later. And we discussed May 4, 1983. At that time, Paul was so heavy that he had a special table at the restaurant with a chair bolted to the wall that could hold his weight so he could get in and out of it easily. He brought us course after course, chuckling at our obvious enjoyment. I kept the menu, savoring the rare crawdads that had shed their shells. For Paul, and most of the other chefs involved in That Night, it was about ingredients more than a particular cooking style. Paul loved butter, fresh fish in season, and local produce. There were French and Cajun influences, but there was also Paul's interpretation that we loved. Miss him.

The AIWF flourished during the years I served on the national board. Julia was active and, in reflection, kept the board together. Robert Mondavi was vital, but Julia was the draw and the glue that allowed the AIWF to remain solvent and flourish for a decade. I chaired several of the wine auctions, which helped with revenue, and chaired Julia's eightieth birthday bash at the Hay-Adams hotel in Washington, DC. All these fundraisers went to support the AIWF goals for culinary education; the expansion of local chapters, which grew in the early years; and the *Journal of Gastronomy*, a beautiful portfolio published between 1984 and 1991.

Copia, the Center for Wine, Food, and the Arts would come later, and Julia would ask me again to join a board, which I did. Once again, her name and Robert Mondavi's on the board masthead were critical for launching the ambitious project. It was a $55 million brick-and-mortar tribute to wine, food, and the arts, today home to a branch of the Culinary Institute of America (CIA) and a restaurant—the latter named after Julia, which she allowed with some reluctance.

There were a lot of people on the Copia board far smarter than me, and I left two years before it folded, hoping it would survive the inevitable, but it would not stop bleeding cash. Despite all the talent and financial and artistic

Tor, Julia, and Susan at a AIWF fundraiser

brilliance, it finally failed—wrong place, wrong time, maybe not enough focus on just wine and food. Too many working parts and messages. Those wanting to read more on its rise and fall should read *The House of Mondavi* by Julia Flynn Siler. It is a clear-eyed look at a blurry picture.

Julia, after Copia, donated the kitchen from her PBS show, *The French Chef*, to the Smithsonian Institution, a fine tribute to the Grande Dame, where anyone can visit today. After her husband, Paul, passed (he had "the dwindles," she used to say to me during his last days), she moved full time to Santa Barbara, and I would visit her at her small apartment at Casa Dorinda in Montecito, near Santa Barbara. One of the major cooking-appliance companies built her a small but excellent kitchen that she was proud of. After a long brunch of eggs Benedict (which she loved), lots of bacon, and all the sides, we were sitting in her dining room, and she started to nod off. I watched as she softly put her head on the table and went to sleep. I called for help, which came immediately. When I was convinced that she would be fine, I left, although I was still concerned about her. I got a call two hours later.

"They mixed my meds—I'm so sorry. Please come back, and let's continue the conversation," Julia pleaded. I did, and enjoyed a wonderful conversation filled with politics, gossip, food, and wine. Those were the last moments I would spend with her.

Julia's culinary library did find homes at UCSB, as well as at the University of California, San Diego, and at Harvard. To me, in a funny way, Julia's quest to find these books a home lit the match that started the revolution. The event on May 4, 1983, An American Celebration, put that match to dry wood and started a fire that burns brightly today. One man's opinion, and there are many. I watched one of her early television shows, focused solely on chicken. It was a rerun with guest celebrity chefs, and I was awed by the detail and accuracy of her commentary and her humor. Some say she was a natural comedian, but we know her to be much more complex—she shared a comedian's intuitive insight into human nature. She made the complicated simple and entertaining and invited us to join her. She championed the home cook and inspired the pros.

Madeleine Kamman was, in many ways, Julia's antithesis. She was also brilliant and perhaps the greatest culinary teacher of my generation. Debatable, but there is a clear argument here, and by opening up her life, I hope to give nuance to the chapter's focus on the Culinary Revolution. To assist me, I asked Gary Danko, one of her students and one of America's top chefs for several decades now, to shine the light on Madeleine, who is sadly forgotten by many culinary historians. Much of the blame for this rests with Madeleine herself, certainly not with a career full of accomplishments.

What follows is a brief history of this extraordinary woman from her Wikipedia page, and a few insider additions.

Madeleine Kamman first learned to cook as a young girl at her aunt's Michelin-starred restaurant in Touraine, France. She returned to Paris at the end of World War II with the hope of attending university, but finances required her to work. She later attended Le Cordon Bleu in Paris, and in 1959 met an American, Alan Kamman. They married and moved to Philadelphia, but by her own admission, she did not easily adjust to life in the United States, in part because she found American cooking and ingredients in the early 1960s inferior to those of her native France.

Madeleine suffered from depression but used cooking as an antidote, and started giving cooking classes in 1966. In 1968, she moved to the Boston area and opened a cooking school, the Modern Gourmet, with a restaurant, Chez La Mère Madeleine, staffed by students from the cooking school. The restaurant received five stars from the Boston Globe, four stars from the Mobil Guide, and accolades from French chef Paul Bocuse. Madeleine closed Chez La Mère Madeleine and the Modern Gourmet cooking school in 1980 to return to France, where she launched a cooking school in Annecy. Her time in France was brief: France's high taxes and what she saw as rampant sexism in France's professional kitchens led her to return to the United States, where she first opened her cooking school in 1984 and Auberge Madeleine on January 29, 1985, a restaurant in Glen, a village of Bartlett, New Hampshire.

In the late 1980s, a diagnosis of heart disease caused her to close the restaurant, and it was around this period she called Tor Kenward at Beringer for help. He visited her at her home in New Hampshire and over a week they mapped out the framework for the School for American Chefs at Beringer Vineyards, a highly competitive two-week training session for professional chefs. Tor made sure it would fit Beringer's hospitality framework and had the company's approval. Madeleine was in charge of curriculum and running the school. In addition to cooking classes, chef-students were given lessons in kitchen chemistry and science, culinary history, geology, and geography to increase their appreciation of menu planning and terroir.

Kamman retired to Vermont in 2000 to pursue a graduate degree in German literature. She passed away in 2018 at the age of eighty-eight.

In addition to her teaching and writing, Kamman created Madeleine Cooks, a PBS cooking show that ran from 1984 to 1991. She received an honorary doctorate from Johnson and Wales University, a Lifetime Achievement Award from the International Association of Culinary Professionals, and a Knighthood in the Ordres des Arts et des Lettres from the French Ministry of Culture, among other awards.

James Beard Awards
Winner, Time Conscious, 1974
Winner, Who's Who of Food & Beverage in America, 1986
Winner, Cookbook of the Year, 1998
Winner, General Cookbook, 1998
Winner, Lifetime Achievement Award, 1998

Some of you may be asking, "Why have I never heard of her until now?" Good question, and not an easy one to answer, but I will try to fill in a few blanks found in this Wikipedia bio, with personal stories that may address the question and illuminate this brilliant woman.

Gary Danko's journey to meeting and finally working with Madeleine is worth telling here. He was graduating from the Culinary Institute of America (CIA) in Hyde Park and wanted a satisfying answer to exactly why hollandaise sauce separated. His instructor gave him a brief and unsatisfying answer. Gary collected cookbooks and copperware, and in one of Madeleine's books, *The Making of a Cook*, he found five pages devoted to the question. As he told me later, "After reading her explanation, I knew I had to work with her."

Gary called her and tried to see her personally, but the answer was always no. Gary persisted, however, and finally heard her reasoning: "You are CIA trained, and I would have to spend too much time untraining you for it to work. Sorry." But Gary finally won her over. It changed his life, and later, mine and all those who have enjoyed Gary's restaurants the last three decades in the San Francisco Bay Area.

I first met Madeleine through Mary Risley, a brilliant cooking teacher in the Bay Area, a no-nonsense, highly respected instructor who asked me to teach one of her classes on wine and told me Madeleine would be visiting her. (Mary had studied under Madeleine in France.) "She loves wine and the people who make it. You should throw a party in her honor in Napa." And I did. It was a great success—many vintners knew of her, especially the women who had their own private cooking schools and culinary-appreciation groups. I told Madeleine I had built scholarship programs with Johnson & Wales University in Rhode Island and the California Culinary Academy, and before I finished the sentence, she said, "Well, you should have one with me."

You don't say no to Madeleine without a heated debate, so I said yes, we would be in touch. A month later, she informed me she was sending me her first pupil. I did not have room in my program, and again, sensing no was not an option, somehow, we made it work. We agreed that her first chef would stay three months and work with us on wine-and-food pairing, in the process cooking for special events. Management particularly liked the program, for it provided a chef for the price of room and board. This was soon to end.

Gary Danko arrived fresh from her school, and his first meal was on a level with those I'd experienced at French Michelin-starred restaurants. This level of cooking stayed with Gary during the three months, and I was convinced we needed to keep him as long as we could. We did—for six years. Two of

those years, he ran the fine dining restaurant at Chateau Souverain, which was owned by the Beringer Wine Estates group at the time. Gary, in his first year running the restaurant, made the cover of *Wine Spectator*'s restaurant edition. It was a true destination restaurant in the wine country, on par with a Michelin-starred country inn. Like Copia, ahead of its time.

Before we opened this very ambitious restaurant, I called my friend John Wright. John was CEO of Domaine Chandon and ran a fine-dining restaurant on the property. "You're going to lose money from the beginning. It is a marketing tool, nothing else. Get used to it." Management never did, and we closed the fine-dining restaurant after two magnificent years.

Gary returned to work with me at Beringer until he left to run fine dining at the Ritz-Carlton in San Francisco, putting the dining room on the gourmet trail and winning numerous awards. I encouraged him to leave us, knowing he needed to be where the critics and foodies could experience his talent without having to visit a winery. He needed to be seen and his cooking experienced by the masses. He cooked for my wedding, numerous birthdays, and so many extraordinary special events at Beringer that we owe him a huge thanks. On a special occasion, Restaurant Gary Danko is on the top of our list.

But back to Madeleine and her Napa Valley adventures. Through the eighties and into the nineties, Madeleine sent me several exceptional chefs to help with Beringer's growing hospitality programs. When we were ready to build out a kitchen for entertaining and teaching, Madeleine visited Napa Valley and helped us with the design. In the back of our minds and over dinner conversation, the question would often come up: "Would she, could she, teach at Beringer?"

I finally flew to New Hampshire to explore how a Madeleine-taught school might work in Beringer's newly designed kitchen. Within a week, Madeleine had in her mind what this would be, and said yes. It was on.

Over the next twelve years, she taught the Madeleine methods to students (many already professional chefs) at Beringer's Hudson House. History, geology, geography, food chemistry, and precision-cooking methods. She was very exacting, hard, demanding, and could bring some students to tears. She

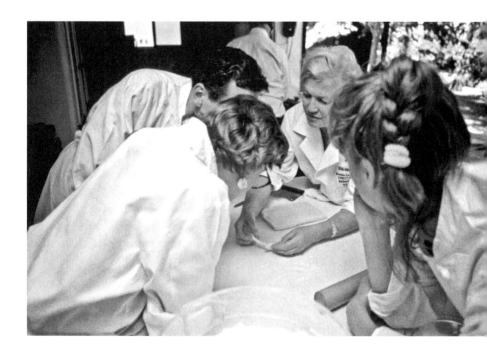

MMK with her students

demanded perfection, full attention to what she was teaching, or you were wasting her time. Though it sounds hard, I have letters of praise and thanks and affidavits of lives changed forever for the better.

Janet Fletcher wrote an excellent piece about Madeleine's retirement from Beringer in the *San Francisco Chronicle* in 2000, worth googling if you want to know more about her legacy as a teacher and writer. Television personality Joanne Weir, Gary Danko, Jimmy Schmidt (who cooked the dinner on May 4, 1983), and numerous others will quantify that she is indeed the greatest teaching chef of our lifetime.

I consider two of Madeleine's books, *The Making of a Cook* and *When French Women Cook*, vital, important additions to any serious chef's library. Julia opened the culinary door first to American minds, hearts, and kitchens through television and her books on French cooking. She inspired the home chef. Madeleine came later and focused on the young chef hungry to be the best professional chef possible. She watched Julia become the spokesperson for French cuisine in America. As Julia's popularity grew, Madeleine became resentful and at times angry. They wrote seminal cookbooks and had long-running cooking shows on television, but Julia was known to millions, and Madeleine, in comparison, only a few.

The war between the two was very public, nasty at times, and heartbreaking to all of us who knew them both. They never did settle their differences. Madeleine built restaurants from scratch and made them great restaurants worthy of Michelin stars. Julia's restaurant was on TV, and her audience was massive. She was pure inspiration for millions of home chefs. Madeleine focused on the professional chef and the serious home cook. Her audience was much smaller and defined.

Madeleine, scoffing at the title of Julia's TV program, *The French Chef*, could never forgive Julia for her celebrity status: "She is not French, and she is not a chef." Later, Julia would respond in her own way, as quoted in Jan Bartelsman's *Magic in the Kitchen*: "I've never had my own restaurant, I know too much about it, and I'm too old now! Anyway, I'm not a chef; I'm a cook and a teacher. We use the term *chef* very loosely in this country."

When I would meet Julia, occasionally, she would ask, "How's that French woman?" I would say "Fine," and we would move on to another conversation. Julia would later repeatedly aver that she wasn't French, nor a chef, but a cook. A chef commanded restaurants and staff. If we were dining at a restaurant, Julia would normally go back to the kitchen and talk with the chef, genuinely interested in them and complimentary. They would never forget those moments.

Madeleine rarely entered a restaurant kitchen unless it was run by someone she knew or had taught. My sense was that if she did, she would tell them immediately what was wrong with the meal and how to fix it. I heard her dissect menus and chefs on nights out. In my mind, she earned the right. Her past was always with her.

Madeleine survived the war in occupied France, where she helped bury the silver and china from her aunt's Michelin-starred restaurant to hide it from the Germans. Tough economic times after the war created food shortages as well as a French restaurant system that was blatantly male-centric at the height of her powers. Three-star chef and celebrity Paul Bocuse would proclaim that women should be in bed, not working in a restaurant. "I was speaking only for myself when I said that I would rather have a pretty woman in my bed than behind a stove in a restaurant. I prefer my women to smell of Dior and Chanel than of cooking fat." Bocuse was quoted in *People* magazine on September 6, 1976: "Women are good cooks, but they are not good chefs." After reading this, Madeleine went to his signed picture in her restaurant and turned it upside down, never to set it right again.

She had been denied so many opportunities (along with many other women chefs), but she was a fighter, and her books alone are an extraordinary legacy. To everyone she trusted with her emotions, she would write us long letters, streams of consciousness, that read like confessionals. She was complex, honest to herself, wounded, and wonderful. Three hundred sixty degrees—a full circle traveled.

In her tome, *When French Women Cook*, she wrote, "Where are you, my France, where women cooked, where the stars in cooking did not go to men anxious for publicity but to women with worn hands stained by vegetables peeled, parched by work in house, garden, or fields, wrinkled by age and experience. Where are you?" She was writing to her true audience, the one that ruled her heart—the French women who fed generations and inspired them to be great chefs.

After Madeleine passed, I received an invitation from Jim Nassikas's son, Bill. Jim had hosted the An American Celebration event at the Stanford Court in 1983. Bill had kept his father's legacy alive in Arizona by opening the Boulders and four other first-class resorts with award-winning culinary

If God forbade drinking, would He have made wine so good?

—CARDINAL RICHELIEU
FRENCH MINISTER, 1585–1642

programs. He wanted me to stay at one of the new properties on my upcoming business trip and have dinner with some restaurateurs and chefs we both knew.

When I arrived in my room, there was a bottle of Champagne on ice from the head chef and culinary genius for many of Bill's properties, Charles Wiley, with a card and a picture attached. The card was a thank-you for playing a role in opening the School for American Chefs and allowing him to attend. The picture was of his class around an al fresco lunch table with Madeleine at the head of the table. She looked very happy in that picture. We all looked so young.

At dinner that night, Bill and the other chefs looked back through the decades we had known each other and the changes American cuisine had gone through since the Big Bang on May 4, 1983, at the Stanford Court.

It was a good night. We drank and dined well—not as extravagant as in some nights past, but very well. The company made up for anything lacking. I felt I had walked a very large circle by the time I made it back to my room.

Reminiscing, I guess I had.

Julia would have liked that night, and she would have started with a martini.

Madeleine would have liked it as well, and she would have started with a glass of Champagne.

Maybe that night they would have made up. Julia was once widely quoted as saying that she might grab Madeleine by the hair and finish her off in a Cuisinart. I was not there when that rumor was born. Both Gary Danko and I noticed when visiting Julia at Casa Dorinda near Santa Barbara that she had one of Madeleine's cookbooks in her library. As Gary noted, "I don't think it was signed."

We are complicated creatures. Working with Madeleine, Julia, and Gary— those were some of the happiest days of my life.

Wine is sunlight, held together by water.

—**GALILEO GALILEI**
*ITALIAN MATHEMATICIAN, ASTRONOMER,
AND PHYSICIST, 1564–1642*

SEPTEMBER

HARVEST. CRUSH. PANDEMONIUM. Prayers. Hope. Little sleep, more chocolate and beer. Yes, it is often said, deep in the belly of the wine country, beer makes wine. Many winemakers, most often the ones that do the hard labor of winemaking, do drink varying amounts of beer while making wine. The winemakers who call the work orders in for others to do the work drink less beer. We all pray for good outcomes. We are united in this universal wine country prayer—let's get these babies in.

When do we pick? This is an important question, and not every winemaker approaches it the same way. Some rely more on the lab numbers—we are all running them—checking sugars, acids, pHs, and numbers that give us an idea of grape maturity. We are all following the weather reports—concerned about storms, heat, conditions that will affect the pick date. The day and time you choose to pick is one of the most important decisions you make as a winemaker, in my opinion. If you miss the window, the wine will know it and will never forgive you. If you hit it, you can proudly show off that wine for decades.

What is that window? At TOR, we do pay attention to the numbers, but equally important is how the grapes and seeds taste. After a few decades, you can lock in on flavors that trigger a pick date by paying attention to how the seeds taste. Are they bitter, or are they becoming more nutlike and less bitter? In my experience, very green, bitter, and tannic seeds do not make good wines. At least, not the type of wines we make at TOR.

I find it amusing how many winemakers pay attention to when their peers start picking. Some don't admit it, but most will when talking among themselves. We are all curious. Pick dates are important because they influence our wines so much. "Who's picking earlier this year? Who's picking later? Why?" We have our own windows in mind, but we pay attention to the winemakers we respect. This same curiosity will be reflected later when we assemble blind tastings with our peer group's wines.

Secret to success: don't ever approach harvest with a hard definition of what you will do. Mother Nature will dictate that. Pay attention to everything around you—the weather, your years of experience working small pieces of land, the look of the vines, the health of the shoot tips, and so on. Be humble, receptive to change, and make sure the winery is completely ready to receive your grapes when you've decided to pull the trigger.

Showtime. The floors are scrubbed, the tanks are spotless, and the barrels are steamed, smell great, and are receptive. It's showtime.

A WINE'S FIRST DUTY IS TO BE RED—UNLESS IT'S WHITE

There are many extraordinary white wines, that, like Rodney Dangerfield said, don't get no respect—at least, the respect they deserve. They are often misunderstood, misplaced, and misused. They are overchilled until you can't smell or taste them, paired with the wrong foods, often introduced at the wrong time, and verbally abused by the uninformed or less adventurous. I don't make white wine to try and change all this—I'm too old for that game. I make white wine because I like to drink it and share it with my friends.

September and October in this book rightfully belong to winemaking and winemakers. So, let's start with a little discussion of white wines. Let's clear some of the cow pies off the field and get it ready for play. In October, we will take on the red wines.

WHAT TEMPERATURE SHOULD THE WINE BE?

This is important and not given enough thought in most cases. For me, a wine's enjoyment diminishes when it or the room I'm enjoying it in is over 75 degrees. It's sacrilegious, I know, but I'll put an ice cube in a red wine that is warmer than 80 degrees, or better, dump the bottle in an ice bucket. White wines are often drunk too cold. Have you ever smelled ice cream? When any beverage is too cold, its aromas and delicate flavors are lost, unless, like ice cream, it is very sweet.

PS: Within an hour, the temperature of your wine will be the temperature surrounding you. Remember that and prepare.

Let's kick off this adventure in white wines—particularly Chardonnay—by making a trip to the Holy Grail of wineries: Domaine de la Romanée-Conti (DRC). Le Montrachet, their Chardonnay, is served after all the red wines on any occasion. It gets respect, huge respect. It can sell for more than $8,000 a bottle—if you can find one. A unicorn white wine if there is one.

Between 1981 and 1992, I visited DRC on three occasions to taste the wines with the winemaker, André Noblet, but more to understand why the wines were so expensive, so revered. What made them different from other white and red Burgundies that sell for a fraction of the price? I was a vice president at Beringer Vineyards, owned by Nestlé in those years, and we were a large importer of wines from Europe, which gave me entry into this holy shrine of wine.

I look back on the notes I took while talking with Noblet. Winemaker to winemaker, he told me he was using Allier Tronçais barrels, although he had tried Vosges, Limousin, and other coopers. He replaced the corks on the old wines in his large library of unlabeled bottles every thirty years. His Le Montrachet was pressed directly to the barrel with much of the solids intact, then barrel fermented; racking was very limited, with less stirring, not much different from his exalted peers. After malolactic fermentation, the wines were moved gently, if at all, but this was true with all the best producers I talked to. Nothing new that would separate him greatly from this peer crowd. I pressed him: "Why are your wines different, or perceived so, from other great Burgundies? They are different, no?"

Noblet, who looked and dressed more like a farmer than a winemaker and whose Pinot Noirs go for over $1,000 a bottle, was very unpretentious in attitude as well as appearance. He paused before answering then shrugged his shoulders. "I believe it is the microflora in our vineyard that might make the difference. Each section of each vineyard has different cultures. We know this. Thousands of years are represented in these populations in our vineyards. They are different from our neighbors. We make our wines using this very specific microflora/yeast population, and this might be what separates us the most from others."

My notes reflect that I wasn't overly impressed with his answer. Today, I am. Today, I'm a believer in natural yeast fermentations, yet their significance is debated by some like the Bordeaux Sciences Agro. On that visit, I was more impressed with the wines we tasted: Romanée-Saint-Vivant, Échezeaux, La Tâche, and the final pièce de résistance, Le Montrachet. It was my favorite wine of the tasting. Thank you, André.

A little side note on André: if you were traveling with an attractive woman, he would spend much more time with you explaining his art and opening bottles. I learned this early on when a group from Hollywood showed up

Winemaker André Noblet in his winery, Domaine de la Romanée-Conti, in Burgundy, pontificating on making wine

with three movie stars at the same time I was in the cellar. His attention was very quickly diverted, and he did open more bottles of wine that day than during my solo visit before.

Four decades later at TOR, we follow André's advice and rely on the natural microflora of each vineyard to give our Chardonnays their stamp, uniqueness, and personality. We give it respect. We make all our Chardonnays the way André made his, and they're probably the same as winemakers before André at DRC. Pick cool, press "dirty" to barrel-cool, primary and secondary (malolactic) fermentations with each vineyard's natural yeast populations, the vintage dictates the sur lies regime, all vintages bottled unfiltered and unfined. There is room for a lot of nuances within those parameters, but this is how Burgundy has made white Burgundy for centuries and still is doing so today. Some things don't need to change in the world of winemaking. This is one.

Many of the broadly US-marketed Chardonnays in the late seventies and early eighties were made by wineries like Robert Mondavi, Beringer, and Jordan, all popular at that time. These wines were fermented in stainless steel, not in small oak barrels, as they did in Burgundy. After primary fermentation, they went to the barrel. Most of these were fined and or filtered. Modern winemaking loved the temperature control of stainless steel jacketed tanks, and it was embraced in California as the Chardonnay frenzy began in earnest in the late 1970s. Small wineries, like Hanzell and others, which always barrel fermented their Chardonnay, were in the minority and continued barrel fermenting, embracing more of the Burgundian techniques.

In 1979, I asked Beringer management to try barrel fermentation on Chardonnay. What greatly supported my plea was a research paper, written by Dr. Vernon L. Singleton from University of California, Davis, on barrel fermentation and the integration of oak in the process. I had heard about his research through the winemaker's underground, so I called him. He picked up, we talked at some length on the subject, and he allowed me to read the treatise. It clearly argued that barrel-fermented Chardonnay integrated the oak flavors far better than fermenting in steel and racking to new, raw barrels.

In my early years at Beringer, they allowed me to work my schedule around classes at UC Davis in winemaking and viticulture. Somehow, I also managed a two-year viticulture degree in one year while still working full time at Beringer. I was obsessed with information and poured this into the *Beringer Vineyard Report*, a newsletter I wrote and we published from 1979 to 1985. It was well received by the winemaking community and consumers on the mailing list. It was the perfect place to introduce Singleton's research, which I did in the February 1983 issue.

Barrel-fermented Chardonnay started to shift slowly at Beringer. Ed Sbragia, the new winemaker, led the charge by creating exceptional wines in the traditional barrel-fermented Burgundian manner. His 1994 Reserve Chardonnay was the #1 Wine of the Year in *Wine Spectator's* Top 100 list in 1996. This was a first for a Chardonnay. The times were quickly changing.

Looking back, it's hard to believe Chardonnay did not appear in the California grape-crop reports in the mid-twentieth century; the reports mixed it in with the reds. It wasn't until the sixties and the seventies that small producers saw there was consumer interest in Chardonnay. One of the most popular, when I started tracking California Chardonnay in the early seventies, was called Pinot Chardonnay.

A decade later, California couldn't plant it fast enough to keep up with demand. This is often a recipe for disaster, and in some respects, it was for Chardonnay. Over the following two decades, a lot of mediocre Chardonnay was made. Some great, but a whole lot of bad Chardonnay, in my opinion. It became a cocktail more than a wine, and this severely damaged the grape's reputation.

Author and über wine educator Kevin Zraly stated it well: "California Chardonnay was the 'it' drink of the eighties, especially for women, becoming a brand as much as a grape." Brands like Kendall-Jackson and Rombauer made versions that were sweet, having a little residual sugar, and sold hundreds of thousands of cases of these concoctions that some sommeliers called cougar crack. No wonder so many guys with average testosterone levels still say to me, "I don't drink Chardonnay."

The specter of many of these "cocktail" Chardonnays still clouds the image of truly great California Chardonnays. We haven't made a Chardonnay that sells for more than $8,000 a bottle like a DRC Le Montrachet. However, if you ever get your hands on this fabled wine, please brown-bag it and go blind against one of California's best. It might surprise you in style and character. Unlike many great white Burgundies characterized by bracing acidity or "brightness" and "minerality" (which can often be sulfide driven), the DRC Le Montrachet is much more California in style. Or you might say great California Chardonnays are Le Montrachet in style. Perception in the wine business dictates reality.

Author and wine legend Michael Broadbent once commented, "White Burgundy (Chardonnay) reflects the perfect union of grape variety, soil, and climate, and at its best epitomizes the summit of the winemaker's art." Michael had his share of great white Burgundies in his lifetime and should know—most all were barrel-fermented, had minimal handling, and were guided by a winemaker who knows when to interrupt the dance and when to let the music keep playing. I barrel fermented my first Chardonnay in 1981 as an experiment at Beringer. Since 2002, Jeff Ames has made all our TOR Chardonnay, and both of us are still learning the dance.

Jeff and I are very clear on how critical the grower is to our success, and Michael points out how important the soil and climate are to the grower. If the grower is not on the top of his or her game, and the location is not ideal, you will never get to the starting gate. The most respected Chardonnay grower I know in California is Larry Hyde. And serendipitously, he is connected in several ways to Domaine de la Romanée-Conti. The joint venture between the de Villaine family of DRC and California is connected at the hip with Larry and his vineyard in Napa's Carneros. Larry's cousin Pamela F. de Villaine is married to Aubert de Villaine. It's all in the family.

Larry, now in his seventies, had a stroke when he was thirty-six. He walks slowly with a cane and is somewhat bent. He looks at you more from the corner of his eyes than straight on, which can give the impression he is appraising you. You feel you are in the presence of wisdom, so you listen closely when he speaks. When we are talking about wine and winegrowing,

| Larry Hyde and his vineyard

wisdom rules. Other than drinking wine with friends and family and growing grapes, he seems happiest when driving his Polaris through his vineyard with his German shepherds in pursuit. The dogs know every vine in the vineyard by now, as does Larry.

Larry purchased this famous Carneros vineyard in 1979, and it expanded to 200 acres in 2020—the year he was named Napa Valley's Grower of the Year by the Napa Valley Grapegrowers (NVG). Larry's vines have become synonymous with many of California's most famous and highest-scored Chardonnays. Over a dozen wineries proudly designate *Hyde* on their label. This designation is highly prized by everyone in the worldwide Chardonnay community. His fame and reputation are built on two cornerstones: terroir and meticulous selection of plant material or clonal selection, which he nurtures, propagates, and builds an international reputation around. All these are available and cataloged at UC Davis's Foundation Plant Services. Larry has made it easier for other growers to share his success. Some of these clones would have been lost forever without Larry's intervention.

In the world of grape growers, especially when it comes to Chardonnay, Larry has few peers. The operation is now Larry Hyde & Sons, with son Chris running the daily operations and business. Larry's wife, Beta, is by his side most every time I visit. They met in 1981 while working in the vineyards in Burgundy for DRC. It is a family-run business from top to bottom—no mysterious partners standing in the wings.

Larry and Chris treat their vineyards like a garden, with beehives and border plantings that encourage a healthy, supportive microflora and insect balance. I annually beg for their honey, which seems to ward off bad spirits, and tastes unlike any other honey I have ever had. The secret sauce to his success as a Chardonnay grower is all this attention to detail, and his knowledge and selections of clones or the vast garden of Chardonnay plant material he covets. All Larry and Chris grow are heritage clones that found their way to California from Burgundy, many as cuttings illegally smuggled in suitcases over the decades. Different selections of early Wente and Calera are Hyde's bread and butter.

Most of California is planted to clones designed to set larger crops. Many of these are Dijon clones that were introduced a few decades ago in Oregon and California. We have worked with some of the Dijon clones over our twenty years of making Chardonnay, and in all our blind tastings, we have always preferred the clones Larry has helped preserve in his vineyard. Dijon clones seem more successful in Oregon—less so, to my taste, in California.

Even though I consider Larry a friend, I had to stand in line for my first block of Wente-clone, small-berry Chardonnay. While I bugged him mercilessly (and enjoyed the honey from the vineyard), he pointed me down the road, where his friend Steve Beresini had taken his prized cuttings and planted a three-acre vineyard in 1984.

"I'd known Steve for a long time as a friend, and he came to me wanting budwood for his property just down the road from us," Larry told me. "The vines he selected were the slyest bearing on the ranch, which at the time amused me. Most growers want higher-yielding, healthy vines. Steve wanted the opposite. Now I see his madness. Small crop, small berries, big flavors in the wine."

I had to try and make a wine from this Beresini vineyard, and we did in 2010. It was the best Chardonnay we had ever made, and we have since taken over all the Chardonnay he grows in his tiny, hand-farmed vineyard. When a vine dies, Steve replaces it with a new plant from cuttings from the old vines. It is his garden.

"The vines I gave Steve are an old Wente clone that originated from the now-defunct Linda Vista nursery," Larry explained. "It is the clone I have in my older blocks. The berries are extremely small and shot clustered. You can never make much wine from these cuttings, and they are known for their minerality and distinct flavors." The Hyde de Villaine (HdV) Comandante bottling comes from the mother block with this old clone. It is the marque Chardonnay of their joint venture.

Finally in 2013, Larry let me into an old Wente block on his ranch (which

some call Hyde Wente) to make wine. Larry told me the cuttings originated
from the old Wente Vineyards in Livermore and had never been "cleaned up"
or heat-treated for viruses. We rarely get more than two tons per acre, but we
love the bright acidity and distinctive quincelike flavors this clone gives a wine.

Another highly praised clone in "Larry's Garden" is the Calera. For any
student of California Chardonnay, the Calera clone means Josh Jensen, one
of the great pioneers of California Chardonnay and Pinot Noir. His Calera
winery was built around his prized vineyard in the middle of nowhere.

I've known Josh for decades and always enjoy the time when our paths
cross. Tall and lean, he once rowed for the Oxford team before taking prized
suitcase vines from Burgundy and planting them in the Gabilan Mountains,
west of Chalone in San Benito County. There's not much in that part of the
world, except the limestone-rich soil and climate Josh believed would make
wines to rival the best in Burgundy. Over the last three decades, many have
done just this.

Larry was given his first Calera cuttings from the vineyard manager, Steve
Doerner. So he calls them his Calera clone. It's that simple. Curiously, the
clusters and berries are larger than the Wente clones in the vineyard, but the
cuttings are highly prized by winemakers like Mark Aubert.

We started to work with a Calera block in Larry's garden in 2019. We
immediately fell in love with the textural material and the richness of the
wine. It was distinctly different from the Wente clone wines we made from
the same ranch—not better or worse, just dramatically different. Our initial
plan was to bottle two wines from the Hyde vineyard, until we went down a
rabbit hole one day in 2020, playing with both wines in the cellar.

Neither Jeff Ames nor I ever thought we would blend a Chardonnay from
two vineyards or different clones. It isn't something winemakers do as they
would with Cabernets. Altogether, we've made Chardonnay for over sixty
years, and the very best Chardonnays we have ever tasted have always been
from single vineyards and single clones. End of story.

End of story—until, in the middle of a pandemic, Jeff and I started to play around and explore what would happen if we went against convention. We worked with blends from Hyde (both Wente and Calera) and Beresini (old Wente) vineyards. The family tree on all these wines, first generation, was from Hyde's vineyard. Before that, the second generation traced back to cuttings from Burgundy, suitcase cuttings from pioneers like Jensen, and first-generation Wente growers.

After numerous tastings, we felt that all the wines stood on their own as exceptional expressions of Chardonnay. But there was one wine—two-thirds old Hyde Wente and Calera and one-third Beresini old Wente—that added another gear and other layers of flavor. It wasn't bigger or broader; it was almost a nod to modern white Burgundy. Thus, the birth of TOR HS Hyde Selection Chardonnay. The HS is our Indiana Jones of Chardonnay—exploring, finding treasures, and bringing it home to the New World.

PS: we released this first TOR HS Chardonnay bottlings in 2021 and sold out in a few hours. Only ninety cases. Price: $155—far less than DRC Le Montrachet, but expensive for a California Chardonnay. There are obviously many people who do drink Chardonnay, who know it can be more than cougar crack, and who give this white wine the respect it deserves.

Combined, we make very little Chardonnay from Larry and Steve's gardens. There are others like Hyde de Villaine (HdV, the joint project with DRC ownership), Mark Aubert, Dave Ramey, and a handful of others who make more and show off the exceptional quality of these grapes. I also invite you to explore the Chardonnay vineyards and winemakers of the Sonoma coast, Monterey, and Santa Barbara County. The top wines, as Michael Broadbent stated, epitomize the summit of the winemaker's art.

In retrospect, many of the best of these great whites are still made as they have been for centuries in France. Several decades ago in California, we tried to improve them with modern equipment and failed in some respects. New presses and gentle pumps aside, we went back in time to find our way home and forward. Even the new, cutting-edge equipment replicates the past. Time has stood relatively still in most Burgundy cellars as well as in the California wineries making old-world-style Chardonnay.

At TOR, we press gently to barrel, ferment in barrel, age, and bottle these Chardonnays unfiltered. Simple. Thank you, Mr. Noblet. Nuances come with experience. Burgundy is always a target for many of us. Both Jeff and I buy wines from domaines we respect and constantly compare them to our efforts. It is getting more expensive each year, but it has to be done.

Work. Work. Work. Yeah, somebody has to do it.

PS: it was a Napa Valley Chardonnay that won the Paris Wine Tasting of 1976.

A DISCLAIMER

I enjoy white wine for so many reasons; even though some may think that "a wine's first duty is to be red," I think differently. White wines get equal standing in my book. Chardonnay, as much as I have championed it in this chapter, makes up more or less 50 percent of the white wines I drink. The other whites I enjoy are not fermented in new French oak barrels. Some are fermented in jars buried in the earth, some in custom amphoras made out of exotic materials, some in stainless steel, some in a variety of sizes of neutral oak barrels, and some in exotic hardwoods. I truly love tracking down wines from all over the world and seeing where the adventure takes me. Yes, I've been disappointed—some of the wines are too acidic or oxidized for my taste—but with the guidance of other international winemakers and friends, I've found great joy.

Another secret for all you cheese lovers: possibly the best wines to enjoy with a wide range of artisanal cheeses are crisp, unoaked white wines. I know that a hunk of spring milk Parmigiano-Reggiano might make your red wine happy, but when you roll up the cheese cart to my table, give me a crisp, unoaked white, and I'll be a happy camper. And it is okay to do this after you've enjoyed some excellent red wines. They do at the Domaine de la Romanée-Conti.

Wine is the divine juice of September.

—VOLTAIRE
FRENCH SATIRIST, AUTHOR, AND HISTORIAN; 1694–1778

*And that you may
the less marvel at
my words,*

*Look at the sun's
heat that becomes
wine*

*When combined
with the juice that
flows from the
vine.*

—DANTE ALIGHIERI
ITALIAN POET AND PHILOSOPHER, 1265–1321

OCTOBER

OCTOBER IS ALL ABOUT PICKING GRAPES, getting them to the winery, crushing, and winemaking. Most of the wines we make in the Cabernet family come into the winery in October. The red fermentations are humming in the tank, whites finishing in the barrel. Long, long days—the longest of the year for the winemaker.

When I came to Napa Valley in the mid-seventies to become a vintner, we had continuous-screw presses, which were much harsher on wines than the presses we work with today. Many wineries in Napa Valley were using large redwood tanks to ferment the red wines. André Tchelistcheff used these at Beaulieu, as did others like Beringer, in the fifties, sixties, and early seventies.

Today's state-of-the-art fermentation tanks have internal pump-overs and temperature controls that, in the right hands, offer winemakers better tools than they had in the past. Pumps have significantly improved moving wine more gently. Computers give us minute-by-minute information on temperature, which helps shape a wine.

Optical sorters have replaced some human hand sorters and make a difference in warmer years, when over-ripeness may affect some of the clusters. A winemaker who works with the newer sorters can precisely dial in the desired grapes. The argument might be made that they are too perfect a machine, eliminating any form of imperfections. In the hands of a well-experienced winemaker, they are helping us make better wines than ever before. There are choices today that we didn't have when I began my journey. Unlike Chardonnay production, which gravitated toward older methods, red wine production has embraced the present and its technology.

Winemakers in Napa Valley continue to experiment with new materials and methods. Concrete fermenters, made out of organic materials from exotic locations, are in vogue with some winemakers for some grape varieties. Napa Valley wines are made in amphoras and in all types of oak, with all types of toast. The array of choices is a smorgasbord for the curious and adventurous winemaker with a big winemaking budget. Postmodern winemaking, natural winemaking, and many other styles and directions are available to any winemaker who chooses to pursue them and has the budget and the ownership vision to explore.

October is that crazy time of year when many of these expensive winemaking toys are taken out of the garage and put to good use. The most amazing part is that after they are used, they go right back into the garage for another year, and they are of no use to the winery except to take up expensive space. Sure, the stainless steel tanks can be used year-round for some wines, but not for Cabernet nor its royal Cinq Cépages family. After fermentation, those wines stay in barrel for their winery life, move on to the bottle, and then find new homes. The equipment we use to crush, press, and make wine in October will be retired before the year ends and put into storage. This drives bean counters nuts, but that is the nature of our business.

October is all about the winemaker nearing the end of act 3. The drama is thick in the air. Time for soliloquies. Time to tie up all the plot points and come to a conclusion.

MAKING GREAT RED WINE IN NAPA VALLEY

First, let's clarify a point: Cabernet Sauvignon is the undisputed kingpin of all the grapes we grow in Napa Valley. Some sommeliers, writers, and critics will occasionally have issues with this, but I'm a historian, and I have been a vintner for the last nearly fifty years, and it is king. Why do some have issues? These minority voices are immersed in the battle for the equal rights of other grape varieties. I get this, because I love variety. Many varieties do extremely well in Napa Valley, but Cabernet is driving the bus and has done so for some time—certainly during all the years of my career. A look back in history gives us context.

After World War II, winemaking and the wines of Napa Valley and Bordeaux went through very dramatic changes, more rapidly than in the past two centuries of winemaking history. Credit for many of these changes goes to Émile Peynaud, who modernized winemaking techniques in Bordeaux. This revolution began in the fifties, accelerated in the sixties, and had a full head of steam into the seventies, when the explosion of wineries took place and hasn't abated in Napa Valley.

What are these changes? Winemakers began to take a closer scientific look at the exact chemistry of winemaking. They had more science, data, and instruments to explore improvements. The most significant of Émile's new winemaking practices was temperature-controlled fermentation, the introduction of stainless steel tanks to accomplish this, inert gases to protect wine from oxidation, and, if needed, sterile filtration to take out the bad bugs. The latter I avoid, but for very commercial wineries making lower-priced wines from below-average grapes, it opened new doors. It made it possible for a sea of inexpensive wines from all over the world to be sold and shipped all over the world. This was not possible before. More important, he stressed a focused approach to understanding which vineyard blocks consistently produced the best wines. Viticulture focused on quality, not just quantity.

It was the Peynaudization of Bordeaux, and it definitely influenced winemaking. Émile stressed the value of ripeness with balance, not green wines made from underripe grapes. It is debatable what the balance in ripeness should be. This will always be a healthy debate, and differences of opinion should be allowed. Over time, the consumer will make the final decision on balance in ripeness. I'm not a fan of green, acidic red wines, and I work hard to target optimum ripeness in each vineyard I work with. Translated, think of that perfect peach at the height of the season, still firm, but with that perfect balance of sugar and acid—so perfect, it almost hurts. This debate aside, Émile revolutionized winemaking in France, and it moved quickly to the United States, to Napa Valley, and finally to all winemaking corners of the world. In Napa, winemakers embraced the good and the bad of Émile's commercial techniques, but creative winemakers like Helen Turley, Tony Soter, John Kongsgaard, and others kept their focus on the good, and particularly, what made the great wines in Burgundy and Bordeaux. They had clarity on the chemistry of winemaking, but their focus was the art and world-class wine.

WHAT YOU SHOULD KNOW ABOUT A WINE LABEL
Where was the wine grown and made, and by whom? All the other stuff is fashion and marketing. Alcohol levels, for some, are very important, but I go by taste. Does it stand out, or is it integrated? Don't rely on the numbers for all the answers.

UC Davis and Fresno State University embraced Émile's scientific approach to winemaking and offered degrees in viticulture and enology. Maynard Amerine was chair of the University of California, Davis, Department of Viticulture and Enology in the fifties and sixties, and he was a dynamic personality, author, and advocate for new systems to grow, make, and judge fine wine. His books were on all our shelves, and his quote "Drink wine, not labels" still resonates. Winemakers like Myron Nightingale, at Beringer, and Louis Martini—both of them graduates from the University of California, Berkeley, class of 1944—sought out science and chemistry classes. Winemaking in California was following science, and the quality of wines from all appellations in all corners of the world began to evolve.

In the seventies and eighties, the top-ranking graduate students in fermentation science or winemaking and enology, stepped into a healthy job market. Gallo and other large wineries poached many of the top graduates. Some also wandered into Napa Valley to become the trailblazers. Men and women worked from the bottom up at wineries like Robert Mondavi in the sixties and seventies—training grounds for the new generation of winemakers. Helen Turley's first job in the Napa Valley was in his laboratory.

Enology degrees with an emphasis in chemistry taught students of the seventies the parameters, the suggested measurements for winemaking. The previous ideal range of the Brix scale, which measures sugar levels, ranged in the low to mid-20s for winemaking, with pH preferably in the low to mid-3 range. Today, those ranges have changed considerably. Brix and pH ranges taught at these universities are not as narrow as when I arrived in Napa Valley in the seventies.

Many celebrated winemakers in Napa Valley today, like Thomas Brown and Jeff Ames, do not have degrees in winemaking and look at winemaking as an organic process. They pay close attention to the science at their fingertips, but they also rely heavily on experience working harvests in Napa Valley or other growing areas under mentor winemakers, find their style, and hone it. Brix ranges are now mid-20s to high 20s, and pHs in the mid to high 3s are normal. The wines have softer tannins, darker colors, more phenolic development, and more flavor.

Out of curiosity, I have run lab numbers on many legendary European wines over the years. The near 4.0 pH on the 1947 Cheval Blanc was an eye-opener, over 14 percent alcohol on Le Montrachet from Domaine de la Romanée-Conti, and Pinots in the 15 percent alcohol range. These wines aged with grace. Another aspect to consider is the learning curve—in winemaking, it extends beyond our lifetimes. We are still learning what works best for wines, and we need the benefit of time to make smart choices in the future.

Two of the most prized books I have in my wine library were written by UC Davis professors and published by the University of California Press. The first book, *Wine: An Introduction for Americans*, by Maynard Amerine and V. L. Singleton, was published in 1968. Maynard lived in St. Helena, and I was fortunate enough to visit and attend tastings at his home. We tasted blind, and he was very precise on how to taste wine and what to look for, and I owe him much for this start. Singleton helped me with a research paper on barrel-fermented Chardonnay, which also altered my life.

My second most prized book, *General Viticulture*, by A. J. Winkler, James A. Cook, William Mark Kliewer, and Lloyd A. Lider, was published in 1974, and it is signed by all four. Working for my degree in viticulture, I became very familiar with this book, and I've read it at least twice. What is taught in both books is dated, but they launched the careers of many great and very influential winemakers and winegrowers since the seventies. In my mind, these books changed the world of winemaking in big and wonderful ways—wines all over the world were just plain better. Regional wines from all over the world, which did not travel well because they were not made properly, were improved with this new knowledge and, for the first time, allowed an international audience. These books taught the fundamentals, which became the base paint for winemaker's canvases. With a good foundation, the best winemakers evolved their own style and signature to their art.

There is a small movement today that feels differently and proselytizes against any interference by humans and science in winemaking. Any. They think of Émile and his concepts as the road to ruin and what UC Davis and Fresno teaches as wrong and interventionist. I think a great winemaker knows when and how to interfere, and when not to, and should use all the tools available to make those choices. For me, an obviously oxidized wine that has lost all fruit has lost its soul. I like to work with equipment that can prevent this from happening.

That said, I have friends interested in wines labeled and marketed as "natural" or "naked" and other marketing names, for each has no clear definition. A few we tasted together had high degrees of oxidation; others had what I viewed as other winemaking flaws. For those friends, these wines are an adventure, and tasting and learning about these wines and how they are made, interests them. So, I step back with the hope we can be true to ourselves and let everyone else find their own paths. Wine allows us many paths, adventures.

Christian Moueix and Joe Heitz are important figures in the modern history of Napa Valley who embraced the science of winemaking at UC Davis and Fresno State, respectively, then turned science into art. The Moueix family is royalty in Bordeaux. At Beringer, we worked with Christian's legendary father, Jean-Pierre Moueix, who after 1950 built an empire of châteaux mostly on the Right Bank—Saint-Émilion and Pomerol. The crown jewel was Château Pétrus, which Christian managed for thirty-eight harvests. In 1983, I visited Pétrus, and I will never forget tasting from barrel the 1982 Pétrus. It was a standout then and tastes young and stunning today. Andy Beckstoffer opened a bottle recently that he shared with me and other vintners. The bottle was a gift from Christian. Small world.

Christian is also a graduate of UC Davis and saw the potential of Napa Valley Bordeaux-style wines early on. Christian founded Dominus Estate in 1982 on a site that was once part of the historic Hopper Ranch and home to many of the great, early Inglenook wines. In 2008, he acquired the Ulysses vineyard nearby. Our paths have crossed many times over the years, lately at Thomas Keller's Bouchon. He just doesn't seem to age with time, nor do his wines. To me, his winemaking style has evolved to be more in sync with Napa, less so with Bordeaux.

Joe Heitz's story goes deeper into the roots of modern Napa Valley Cabernets. He was stationed in Fresno as an army pilot in the forties and began working at a nearby winery in the evenings and weekends; later, he worked at Gallo. In 1951, he moved to Napa and worked under André Tchelistcheff at Beaulieu and focused on Cabernet. In 1958, he and his wife, Alice, moved back to Fresno and helped establish the Viticulture and Enology Research Center at Fresno State. This would become one of the epicenters of modern winemaking, along with UC Davis, over the next century. In 1961, he and Alice moved back to Napa and founded Heitz Cellar.

Heitz Martha's Vineyard wines in the sixties and seventies were the most expensive and revered Cabernets in California. Tom May and his wife, Martha, for whom the vineyard is named, bought their property in the early sixties and have been extraordinary stewards of this vineyard since then. When I moved to Napa in the seventies, I spent some time with Joe and was taught that you don't pick at 22.5 Brix, you pick closer to 25—the same number he liked to give Belle and Barney Rhodes, who planted Martha's and later Bella Oaks vineyards. "I want to get to 25," he would instruct—or shout out, according to Belle—and they listened. Joe was a rebel in some ways, an iconoclast in most, and a brilliant winemaker. His Martha's Vineyard wines are one of the most sought-after wines in Napa history. One reason is that they have aged well and are mind-bending wines to taste today. Napa Valley wines were about to take a large leap, following Joe's exploration into a riper style.

In my eyes, 1991 was another turning point for Napa Valley wines—Cabernet Sauvignon in particular. First, it was an exceptional high-quality vintage, and the best wines have held up extremely well over the decades. Second, the winemakers were paying more attention to the vineyard, and winemaking styles were seeking more extraction, more density, more flavor.

Third and in tandem, it was the unofficial launch of many cult wineries. These wineries, with 100-point endorsements from Robert Parker and scores in the high nineties from Jim Laube, were in such great demand that collectors of these cult wines would purchase their allocations and then flip them immediately for much higher prices on a secondary market. One winery would respond to queries about joining their mailing list with "Sorry. We have a waiting list for our waiting list."

Harlan Estate's first released vintage was 1990, but it released the 1991 first. Bryant, Maya, Screaming Eagle, and others launched around that time and, like the early Beatles, had crazed fans hunting them down. I personally loved the heat and noise the cults were creating. It was a rising tide, and all of our ships were rising in this madness, too. Local winemakers denied being a member of any cult, but we followed them closely and paid close attention to new practices in the vineyard and winery: greater thinning in the vineyards; organic and biodynamic farming; experimental spacing in vineyards; new small, experimental French oak coopers; later picking dates; more extractive winemaking practices. It was the Wild West, and the wines were evolving.

The local wine shop in St. Helena was owned by Fred Beringer (who had sold his part of the Beringer winery to Nestlé). During the beginning of the cult phase, I would wander in regularly to say hello and take the pulse of the new cults he proudly featured. One day in 1994, Fred lamented he had a winery that hadn't received the attention he thought it should. From a case stack near the door, he picked up two wooden three-packs of the wine and dropped them in front of me.

"They're yours. You know the right people to share them with, and I want your honest opinion. We think it's great stuff." I couldn't remember when I had ever turned down free wine, especially in a nice wooden box, so I thanked him and took the wines home with me. The first bottle, I shared with Jim Laube of *Wine Spectator* one night over dinner. The second bottle, I sent to Robert Parker with a nice note asking him to try it. Later, it would get 100 points. The wine was the 1992 first vintage of Screaming Eagle, which now goes for $7,000 and up per bottle. I drank the remaining bottles with appreciative friends. Didn't flip a single bottle. Some questioned my wisdom.

The year Thomas Keller purchased the French Laundry in Yountville from Don and Sally Schmitt, who owned it under the same name—1992— is also significant. Their restaurant was a favorite of locals, but it didn't have much bandwidth outside them and serious foodies. I proposed to my wife there in 1986, and Sally allowed me to put the engagement ring in a dish of fresh oysters.

Under Thomas's direction, the French Laundry in some ways followed the path of the cults. You had to be an insider or an investor to get a table. It reminded me of Alain Chapel's Michelin three-star restaurant, which I visited in France during the eighties. Immaculate service, rural setting, incredible wine list, and the best purveyors in the marketplace. Thomas nailed it, and Napa quickly became a destination for its restaurants and its wines.

Napa Valley in the nineties was the place to be and be seen, it seemed. Celebrity chefs were mingling everywhere. At Beringer, I hosted Charlie Trotter, Lidia Bastianich, Julia Child on several occasions, chefs representing American regional cuisines, such as Edna Lewis (who made killer mint juleps every morning around ten o'clock), and chefs from Japan and Europe. Movie stars, politicians, and sports heroes showed up on a regular basis. At Beringer, we made a joint-venture wine with San Francisco 49ers great Joe Montana. Captains of industry and finance were investing in wineries and building homes. The Meadowood and Auberge du Soleil resorts catered to the high rollers. Mustards Grill and Tra Vigne were the watering holes for casual diners. I had house accounts that got me in trouble more than once.

Winery dream teams came about in the nineties, too. These still exist, but they flourished in the nineties. Billionaires and millionaires wanting to take a

Former secretary of state Colin Powell and Tor talk wine not politics at a dinner in recognition of public-private partnerships for humanitarian demining, November 27, 2001

large fortune and turn it into a smaller fortune hired them to build wineries and make wines that would make their names synonymous with great wine and good taste. Any return on investment, unless they sold to another wealthy hopeful for a higher price, was guaranteed never to happen in their lifetime. Nancy Andrus Duckhorn (married to Dan Duckhorn) was a master of putting these teams together. Scarecrow, OVID, and others called on her to put together their dream teams.

Think of major sport franchises (for example, baseball, football, and soccer teams) when wrapping your head around these dream teams and how they functioned. Marquee winemakers draw attention to the brands, creating excitement. In the eighties and nineties, celebrity winemakers with 100-point wines under their belts were superstars. Some moved around from winery to winery. Some stayed with their early dance partners, but they started piling up their dance cards with new partners.

The first dream team that comes to mind is Helen Turley and David Abreu. David planted vineyards (and made his own cult brand); Helen made the wines. As with many great artists, there are a lot of stories about how difficult it was and is to work with these greats, but put all that aside—they made a whole lot of 100-point wines as a team and separately. I worked with David—we planted a small vineyard together—and I have great respect for him and his team. I've tasted with Helen on several occasions and enjoyed her insights on the wines. Curiously, both are introverts and let their success do most of the speaking.

Another crowned diva, who has taken on many consulting jobs since the nineties, is Heidi Barrett. Heidi was making the wine for Dalla Valle in the early nineties. She bumped into a neighbor, real estate agent Jean Phillips, and agreed to make Jean's wine, Screaming Eagle, in the early years. Alumni Screaming Eagle winemakers include Andy Erickson, who is one of the most successful consultants today in Napa Valley. Screaming Eagle has always attracted the top-tier dream teamers. David Abreu, of course, planted the vineyard and planted again. Current winemaker Nick Gislason, a former Harlan employee, replaced Andy. Michel Rolland works on the final blends with Nick. Nothing but the best for a wine that retails today for $1,150 a bottle on release.

It's hard for me to think of any winemaker who has traveled more on wine projects than Rolland, the Flying Winemaker. Although I've never made wine with Michel, we have played golf together, and I know he takes his work very seriously and has earned his reputation of king of the blend. The last time I checked in, he was consulting for 150 wineries in thirteen countries, and over 400 wineries use his lab for analysis and help. I'm amazed that he tries and maintains a golf game with that schedule, but he

See simplicity in the complicated. Achieve greatness in the little things.

—LAO TZU
CHINESE PHILOSOPHER; SIXTH CENTURY; FROM TAO TE CHING, *CHAPTER 63*

does. The winemakers at Screaming Eagle, Harlan, Dalla Valle, and Bryant, to name a few Napa Valley favorites, praise his skills.

To bring this sketch of Napa Valley winemaking of the nineties into the new century, I need to mention other gifted consultants. A Bordeaux native, Philippe Melka began his imprint in 1995 and has more than thirty clients. Aaron Pott, who I worked with in my Beringer days, and Celia Welch (Scarecrow) are some of the names who have taken the term *consulting* to new heights and have formed many dream-team rosters.

Thomas Brown, another consultant, has forty clients and a waiting list today. Thomas was my first winemaker, and I was one of his first clients. Thomas represents the new wave of winemaking that helped define Napa Valley Cabernet in the twenty-first century. Thomas had no formal winemaking education (from UC Davis, Fresno, or Bordeaux). His early Napa job was in 1996 at the All Seasons wine shop in Calistoga, where he made strong impressions on visiting winemakers. Ehren Jordan gave Thomas his first winemaking job at Turley Wine Cellars in 1997. Ehren was so impressed with Thomas's focus and his ability to handle several tasks at the same time, he handed over his two consulting projects to Thomas to manage shortly afterward. Thomas was a phenomenally quick learner, and though he has a quiet personality, he seemed to always be at occasions where the best bottles were being opened. That is how I met Thomas.

Thomas and his inner circle of friends are lifelong students of the great wines of the world. To me, great winemakers love wine, all great wines, and never tire of exploring different regions and studying what other winemakers are doing. Avocation becomes vocation. Great winemakers rip a lot of corks. In 2000, I set up a dinner in St. Helena for Robert Parker, introducing him to a handful of young winemakers I thought might represent the future. Thomas was one.

I hired Thomas in 2001, and he was my solo winemaker. In 2002, Thomas was expanding his role as a consultant winemaker and hired Jeff Ames and Mike Smith. Jeff was the point person on my project, and, like Thomas, he explored the wide world of wine with diligence and dedication. Thomas, Jeff, and Mike are all cork dorks, love Champagne, Burgundy, Barolos, and Northern and Southern Rhônes, and I had a lot of all these in my cellar. We became friends, and we still are.

In 2003, Thomas came to me and said, "Jeff loves your project and would like to be your full-time winemaker. I'm taking on more consulting projects, and Schrader's a handful. What do you think?" I liked Jeff's hard work ethic, love of wine, and winemaking, so I said, "Let's try it." The year was 2003, and Jeff and I have worked together ever since. Jeff is brilliant, and one of the hardest-working winemakers I know. No, he's actually the hardest working. A man who loves his work, and his wines show it.

What is interesting about both Thomas and Jeff is that they do not like the spotlight on them—both would rather raise a family and make wine than go on a road show. Both are quiet and introspective, and I think I've said this before: they are very passionate about wine, which translates to great winemaking. Jeff's perfect day is spending time with his daughter, then tasting through the barrels, imagining blends, and getting familiar with every barrel we have in the winery. Or standing at a press, tasting young wines, determining by taste the exact moment to stop the press. He doesn't call this in, which some consultants do.

Like Thomas, Jeff came from the South, a Southern boy at heart. Both went to Southern universities, and both gravitated to the West at about the same time, lured by the wine bug. Neither took courses in winemaking, and both chose to work under brilliant winemakers to listen and learn. The choices we make in life can be so random. I occasionally feel we are all pinballs subject to gravity and inertia that takes us places we have absolutely

Jeff Ames's breakfast wine

no control over. Jeff's path to being a winemaker is a good case in point about this random nature that defines our careers and lives.

"I look at my job as a winemaker as a mistake," Jeff says. "I was in grad school at the University of Memphis, preparing to be a lawyer under my father's guidance, and took a night job in a liquor store. The wines I could try opened my eyes to the world." Jeff and I both worked jobs on all our summer vacations from high school and college. Jeff took a job at Harrods in London in 1996 and gained more exposure to the world of wine. When he returned to the university, he entered a master's program in education. He had narrowed his future to teaching children or making wine.

In 1998, Jeff sent his résumé, which had nothing in it to qualify him as a winemaker, to several wineries in California and Oregon. No one replied, except for Lynn Penner-Ash at Rex Hill in Oregon. She said she might have a job—emphasis on *maybe*—and would interview him if he came out. He drove across the country to Oregon and knocked on her door.

"You drove across the country to see me about the 'maybe' job?" She was a bit shocked and amused. "Well, I don't think we have one, but maybe we should if you've come all this way." He was hired and did all the dirty work for the harvest that year. He recalls, "I loved every bit of it."

Over the next two years, Jeff worked the Duckhorn Vineyards tasting room and at an online wine-auction company called WineBid, wrote wine articles for *Decanter*, and did other odd wine jobs to pay the rent. The wine bug was flowing in his veins.

He was also forming friendships with up-and-coming winemakers like Thomas Brown and Tony Biagi. If he had any extra money at the end of the month, he spent it on wine and card games with other winemakers. "They liked playing with me because they took my money. I'm not a good card player," he confesses.

In 2001, when Thomas was making wine for Outpost and Chiarello (Ehren's clients), Jeff joined his team, and I made my first TOR Cabernet with Jeff and Thomas at Outpost in 2001. Jeff has been with me now for twenty years. Our focus has always been single-vineyard Cabernets from vineyards that we knew would be world-class sites. Beckstoffer To Kalon, Vine Hill Ranch Vineyard, Beckstoffer Dr. Crane, Melanson, and Tench we consider Napa Valley First Growths. A classification system in Napa Valley doesn't exist, but it is forming in our minds.

Looking back on our years working together, there was a movement in Napa Valley to make Cabernets that went too far—too ripe, too much toast in the barrels. Just plain too much. At least, that's how Jeff and I viewed them. These Cabernets were the minority, but a few were very famous and not to our liking. To some, these Cabernets gave Napa Valley a bad rap, but others enjoyed the wines. I don't judge. I avoid these wines and focus on those that show off the vineyard, the team that manages the vineyard, and the winemakers who manage the wines.

Jeff and I almost finish each other's sentences when we are talking about the wines we like and the ones we don't. I occasionally view this as a problem, so we open our wines as often as we can to our peers. I get the final say on the blends, but I'm smart enough to listen to everything they say, and more importantly, to Jeff, for he knows every barrel far better than anyone when we get to the final, final blend. We've never included another hired blender like the famous Michel Rolland to our table. I did work with a master of wine, Matt Deller, whose opinion I valued, and since he moved back home to New Zealand, I do miss it. I'd be curious what another blender might think, but we have an A-team that has over twenty years of working together. I do listen closely to what others tell me about our wines, especially the wine critics I admire and respect.

Possibly the greatest asset Jeff and I have is the experience we have with each vineyard and the wines we make from our individual blocks. I will never understand how some brands fire and hire new winemakers every few years, forming new dream teams as they hope for new results.

We launched TOR in 2001, and both of us feel that it wasn't until 2008 that we hit our stride and started making our best wines. All the early wines had excellent reviews and seem to be aging brilliantly, but something came together in 2008 that wasn't there before. Why? Honestly, we knew the vineyards much better than we did when we started and how to best work with the fruit each site gave us. Consistent excellent winemaking is about decades, not months or years.

This hidden no-science element in fine winemaking is experience, focus, and taste memory. I've always felt that if you make a truly great historic wine your first year, you got lucky. Don't count on the luck to follow you around every year after that. It won't. Like a marriage that has grown stronger over time, you learn your strengths, and you work harder on weak points to strengthen them. It is this kind of experience you cannot buy. You have to put in the time.

During the year of the COVID-19 lockdown, wine writers did not travel, so we sent them our wines. They scored them at home, and in most cases, it was the first time in their career as critics that they had time to evaluate the wines over several days. In the past, if they liked a certain wine, they would taste it once, score, and move on to the next winery, forming quick opinions in a narrow space of time. The lockdown gave them a new opportunity to get deeper into their knowledge of the wines and follow those wines that intrigued them over the course of days.

Antonio Galloni, a wine critic and writer whom we highly respect and who has built a solid reputation for tasting (and for his maps of Napa Valley), made this observation. It was a revelation to him, and he wrote about it in his reviews of Napa Valley wines in his newsletter, *Vinous*. Jeff and I videoconferenced with him a few times after he had tasted our wines, and he was very complimentary on how well the wines improved through time. His scores reflected this observation. We witnessed this with other critics during the lockdown. During this year, while showing off the 2018 Cabernets and Cinq Cépages blends, we had seven 100-point scores, four 99-point scores, and ten 98-point scores.

It took over four decades to be an overnight success—as it should be when making fine wine.

| *Jeff Ames and Tor at the winery during harvest*

To take wine into our mouths is to savor a droplet of the river of human history.

—CLIFTON FADIMAN
AMERICAN INTELLECTUAL, WRITER, AND EDITOR, 1904–1999

NOVEMBER

EXHAUSTION CAN SET IN. It's weird, but this can be combined with a form of elation, knowing all the grapes are in and either fermented or winding down and finally going dry. But long days catch up to you, and you are tired to the bone. Occasionally, there are stubborn fermentations that keep you up at night, that slow to almost a stop and worry you that they might not finish. Stuck fermentations happen and are every winemaker's nemesis, for they can be very hard to start again. It is critical that all your fermentations go dry. Looking back on our twenty years at TOR, we've had some scares, but all eventually have gone dry. Good work, Jeff.

Other tools in a winemaker's toolbox that are not often discussed:

Cold-soaking before fermentation can increase the extraction of pigments from the skins, which can increase color and influence flavor.

Extended maceration takes place after fermentation when the wine sits on the skins for days or up to weeks. This can soften tannins in a red wine by increasing the molecular size of the tannins. Small tannin molecules are more bitter. Over our years of winemaking, we have used both techniques, but the vintage will dictate the final call. The temperatures the winemaker ferments the wine from beginning to end can have a great influence on the taste, body, and character of a wine.

These are a couple of the decisions a winemaker faces in November and December. Probably the most important for me is the day the winemaker finally chooses to press the wine to barrel. Whites are pressed before fermentation, reds after. Some winemakers use a certain amount of the harsher-press wine in their red wines for body and flavor. Rarely have we used harsher-press wine, and the moment Jeff chooses to stop the press is very personal and based on all his years of tasting press wine. His decades of experience will greatly influence the final wine two years later, when it is bottled. I enjoy spending time with Jeff at the press. He is the master.

In the vineyard, mid-November into December might be the time some vineyard managers start pruning after a hard frost, when the vines go dormant. This works well for very large vineyards that require a lot of time to prune. All our vineyards are small, and we have crews that know what we want and can do it relatively quickly. All the vineyard crews we work with put pruning off until the beginning of the next year.

The winemaker's year is finally winding down. We've had one more classroom to learn valuable lessons about winemaking and each other. Hopefully, along the way, we've mentored others in the process. This chapter is about finding magic in the wines and learning from the masters and mentors that pass on to us valuable lessons we hold onto for life.

LESSONS IN WINEMAKING—FINDING THE MAGIC

In 2014, we had a massive 6.0 magnitude earthquake that shook Napa Valley at 3:20 in the morning. It was violent—threw a lot of people out of bed, crumbled some structures, and scared the hell out of everyone. No one I know slept through this one. Strangely, some people saw a flash of light during the short period of time the earth shook, which was later attributed to rock below the surface of the earth, like a flint striking against flint, giving off energy. I saw this outside our window. It was like seeing a UFO. You're not really sure you saw it, and your mind tries to deny it, but the picture in your mind is there for life. Frozen in time.

As we wandered around our home, we were happy that very little damage had occurred, and I was elated that the wine cellar was intact. Not a bottle broken. But my huge concern, deep in the pit of my stomach, was the winery—the barrels and the tanks filled with precious, irreplaceable wine. I called Jeff—he was already on his way to the winery. We had no idea what to expect.

When he reached the winery and started to walk to the barrel *chai*, he noticed the first river of wine seeping under the door. What he found inside the chai was shocking, disturbing, frightening. Many of the barrels, which had been stacked atop each other on metal racks, lay whole or broken a few yards away on the floor. A few were located twenty yards away, in pieces. One barrel literally flew into a cement wall and stuck there, lodged and broken. At first glance, this seems impossible, but when you remember that each barrel, when filled, weighs half a ton, realization sets in. I arrived shortly after, crawled as far as I could over broken barrels, the smell of wine on the floor filling nostrils with pure dread. I was numb.

Weeks later, after we topped up all the barrels that had survived and removed the broken ones, we figured that we had lost 20 percent of the red wine vintage for 2013. Some wineries lost everything; some none. It was random destruction and heartbreak. We did not have earthquake insurance—less than 10 percent of the wineries in Napa Valley did. But there was a huge silver lining: if the quake had struck during work hours, there would have been death and human suffering created by those heavy barrel projectiles flying through the air. Thankfully, no lives were lost in the 2014 Napa Valley earthquake.

As a community, we slowly got back on our feet. Everyone I knew was involved in helping the less fortunate, helping to clean up the mess. It took months. It was introspection time for me. Once we had accounted for all the surviving barrels and tasted through them, we found five that we thought might be the best barrels of wine we had ever made from the 2013 vintage. Had the earthquake magically waved a wand and said, "You are the phoenix," a symbol of hope and resurrection to these barrels? It appeared so. We talked about keeping them separate and pondered what we might call the wine if we did.

During this period, I clearly remember sitting on the back porch of our home in St. Helena as the sun went down, a glass of Cabernet in my hand, divining inspiration. Out of nowhere, the sound of Louis Prima and Keely Smith rattled through my head and wouldn't leave: "Old black magic has me in its spell / Old black magic that you weave so well / Those icy fingers up and down my spine . . . " They were going up and down my spine.

The earthquake was a black moment for us at TOR. We lost a lot of great wine, wine that would never make it to the bottle and to our customers. But we did have five barrels, dark as a moonlit night, with an aura of real magic. It was a monumental wine that would be called Black Magic. And it was and is today.

SEEKING PERFECTION WHEN MAKING WINE

Some pursuits are based on the humanly impossible—perfection. Golf and fly-fishing are two I pursue, and occasionally I like to think I hit the perfect shot or made the perfect cast. The results might support this belief with a hole-in-one or a trophy fish, but we all know perfection is an attitude, and all we have is a glimpse of it. A glimpse—that's often good enough for me

The 2018 TOR Black Magic received four 100-point "perfect" scores from leading wine critics. We call it our 400-point wine.

and for some wine critics who give our wines 100 points. Perfection in one moment of time that lives forever on paper or in memory.

Every time we make a Black Magic or any of our wines, we are shooting for that elusive goal called perfection. Blending sessions with my winemakers are right up there with the hole-in-one and trophy trout. There is no other part of the process of making fine wine that excites me and pushes as many of my buttons as blending wines with exceptional single-vineyard material. Nothing. If we nail something big, find a wine we didn't know existed, and exceed the sum of the parts, it is a huge high. I'm an unabashed blending junkie. It is why I have the final say on every blend, every wine.

The 2013 inaugural Black Magic has a backstory. We located our five magical barrels we had set aside and put together even better. But we were seeking perfection, and before we made up our mind on the final blend, we had to exhaust all possibilities to improve the wine. One direction I was very interested in pursuing was adding a little Petit Verdot.

Petit Verdot is one of the five Cinq Cépages grapes planted throughout Bordeaux's many appellations. Each of these grape varieties—Cabernet Franc, Cabernet Sauvignon, Malbec, Merlot, and Petit Verdot—ripens on a different schedule. If they were all together in one vineyard, closely planted together, Petit Verdot would be the last to come in. For this reason, during cool decades in Bordeaux's twentieth century, Petit Verdot was replaced with one of the other varieties because it would not ripen in the cooler years. Now it is making a comeback. Why? When it does ripen, it can—here we go again—be magical.

When added in small amounts, Petit Verdot can add a sexy "mineral" note and an aroma of hot, wet granite or stone that pops the more fruit-driven character of Cabernet Sauvignon. All that said, it is very hard to find great Petit Verdot in Napa Valley. It is not widely planted and doesn't grow as effectively in as many soils and locations as does Cabernet. Some of the best Petit Verdot I had tasted, over my decades of winemaking in Napa Valley, was from the Araujo Estate Wines (renamed Eisele Vineyard Estate) and from the Vine Hill Ranch Vineyard, which they used in some of their blends.

In 2013 the proprietor of Vine Hill Ranch Vineyard, Bruce Phillips, allowed me to buy grapes from a small block of Petit Verdot that resulted in about three tons of grapes or seventy-five cases of wine. The vineyard and its management (led by Mike Wolf) is brilliant, and it is one of the Harlan BOND Winery vineyard designates, Vecina.

I knew Bruce's parents well in the 1980s and felt privileged to work with these grapes. Legendary wines going back to the Beaulieu Georges de Latour Private Reserve bottlings, made by André Tchelistcheff, have showcased this vineyard on the southern border of west Oakville. We now work with three blocks of Cabernet Sauvignon and helped convince Bruce to plant more Petit Verdot.

We've found magic fermenting the Cabernet with the Petit Verdot.

The Petit Verdot (PV) lived up to my expectations, so much so that we felt it could be bottled as pure PV, which is very rare. Or, as it is more commonly used, it would find a home in a Cabernet-based blend. We tried and tried, but nothing really felt even close to our goal of the perfect blend until we tried it in the potential Black Magic blend in 2013. Our first run at this was at 2 percent, and it was exciting at first sniff and taste. However, it wasn't seamless and had an awkward edge at the very end of its life on the palate.

Next, we tried 4 percent; no. Eight percent; no. Twelve percent; interesting, but no. Fifteen percent; really interesting—maybe. Blending a wine can be very counterintuitive. Why would the higher blend and the lower blend be best, and not the ones in the middle? I've learned over many decades of tasting that you just cannot go at making wine with a preset perception. I've seen very experienced tasters make fools of themselves. As a wine blender, you will not guide the wine; the wine will guide you. Allowing this process to unfold and being patient often gives us the greatest rewards.

We tried 20 percent and then tried 2 percent. Two percent won the tasting. We needed to exhaust all possibilities, however, especially since the lower percentage was guiding us again. We tried 1 percent and liked that a little more than the 2 percent. I asked Jeff to make up a 0.5 percent and try it blind against the 1 percent and the wine without the PV. We tasted all three blind. They were all clearly different wines, all excellent in different ways, but we all picked the winner to be . . . the 0.5 percent.

How 0.5 percent of any wine could dramatically change a wine, or even be detectable, may sound impossible, but it clearly was. The 99.5 percent Cabernet Sauvignon and 0.5 percent Petit Verdot became our first Black Magic wine. The vintage was an excellent one marred only by an earthquake. When someone or something knocks you to the ground, it is how you get up that often defines you. I like to think the 2013 Black Magic defined us that year.

Ever since, Black Magic is simply defined as the best wine from the best barrels. We don't make it every year. We make that call. The process of finding "Magic" is exhilarating when you are working with the vineyards we have as partners in crime. Every year we plot to make the Crime of the Century, and this is so much fun for highly skilled criminals who love winemaking. Why would you want to do anything else for a living? It's

Jeff after a productive blending session for TOR Black Magic

like breaking into the Louvre, studying masters close up as long as we choose. No closing time. Round up the usual suspects. It must be illegal or criminal to play as hard as Jeff and I have over the last twenty years and call it work.

A CRIME OF THE CENTURY

The 2016 vintage is viewed as one of Napa Valley's greatest. I've been a part of over four decades of mixed vintages, and I go with the critics on this one. Hindsight is always twenty-twenty when appraising good and bad vintages. Like a few of my peers, I remember them all going back to 1974, when I first visited the valley and started tracking Napa Valley wine. Curiously, many critics touted the 1974 vintage, and, to a lesser extent, the 1975. Today, I prefer the 1975s. The 1978 was a critics' favorite, and again, with time, the best of the 1979s might have edged the favorite 1978s out. I'm not saying the critics are wrong—only that time itself will make the correct call. We are human. Time is divine.

In 2016, which is still waiting for its coronation in time, we had a situation at the winery I had never faced before when making TOR wines. Jeff and I got into a friendly argument about whose outcome could be an expensive mistake. We had picked all the Petit Verdot and a new block of Cabernet from Vine Hill Ranch Vineyard on the same day, and I had planned to ferment them separately. I was very keen on judging the potential of the new block of Cabernet—it showed exceptional promise and had the potential to be outstanding.

Jeff wanted to ferment them together. Jeff's argument was that it would fit nicely into a four-ton tank, and it might "be interesting." Well aware of the cost of grapes involved in this decision, north of $100,000, "interesting" didn't carry the day for me. I wanted to see the potential of the Cabernet, and if we put them together, it would be a wine that would be 55 percent Cabernet Sauvignon and 45 percent Petit Verdot. This high percentage of PV not only made the blend highly controversial and very unconventional, but I also had no idea what to call it—or what to do with it when it approached bottling. What would it taste like? We had no examples of a wine like this in our extensive memory banks. Would it be a Frankenstein wine and terrorize the vintage for us? The proprietor/owner has to think of these things; the winemaker doesn't.

If we had a board of directors and investors who expected a little return on their investment down the road, I don't think the argument would have lasted long. Jeff would have lost immediately. But he didn't, and I kept turning it over in my head as he persisted and sent other winemakers I respected to pound on my cage and support his position. "Take a chance," they were all saying. They had a good feeling about it.

I caved, and we co-fermented the two blocks together in one tank of almost equal amounts of Cabernet and PV. In short, the wine was my favorite wine of the vintage. It was controversial, but I loved it, and so did Jeff and all the winemakers who beat me up, insisting we give it a try. It became the 2016 Black Magic. We didn't blend anything else into it. To us, it was perfect by itself—and, possibly more important, it changed the way we make wine at TOR.

Co-fermenting Petit Verdot and Cabernet Sauvignon at the winery is all we do now. It is rare for us to ferment them separately. After over fifty years of having my head buried in the winemaking game, I never saw this coming. I had looked at the greatest wines made, the height of the winemaker's art being single-vineyard pure Cabernet Sauvignons. In most years, they still may be, but I am working with more of these co-fermentations each new harvest.

Today, we have Cabernet Franc in Beckstoffer To Kalon that we co-ferment with the Cabernet. At Vine Hill Ranch Vineyard, with the help of owner Bruce Phillips, we are planting new blocks of Petit Verdot. This is a bit crazy for a grower who can make more money on Cabernet Sauvignon than PV, but Bruce has tasted the wines and is a visionary. We have a new block of Petit Verdot at the historic Tench vineyard in Oakville and are experimenting with a new block of Cabernet Franc on the Upper Range, a new groundbreaking vineyard in the eastern hills of Napa Valley. We are committed, thumbing our nose at our board of directors (Susan and *moi*) and peering into the future.

Who else is experimenting with co-fermentations? I hear rumors that my friend David Abreu is, but no confirmation. Dave keeps things close to the vest, and I'm sure there are many others. I'm hoping this book brings more out of the shadows. Maybe we will start a club. Maybe not. I'm not

PLAYING FAVORITES

I'm often asked, of all the wines I make, which one is my favorite? I've heard other winemakers dodge the question by stating that all their wines are like their children, and they cannot possibly pick a favorite. Well, I can tell you there are some days when I can pick a favorite child, and some days I can pick a favorite wine. But it does change from day to day.

good at joining clubs. I can speak for us—you can teach an old dog a new trick. Thank you, Jeff, for pushing me over the cliff. The free fall has been exhilarating, and you stuck the landing.

In 2018, the Black Magic and two new Pure Magic wines were made with high percentages of co-fermented wines. Together, they racked up six 100-point scores from the major wine critics—the Black Magic four 100-points alone, which I believe is a record for one wine. We call it our 400-point wine. Some people view this as the end of their journey. For us, it is still the beginning.

LEARNING FROM THE MASTERS: MENTORS

Another highly prized book in my wine library is by Henri Enjalbert, titled *Great Bordeaux Wines*. The book was given to me, and is inscribed by, Christian Moueix (general manager at Pétrus at the time), acknowledging the business relationship we had with the Moueix family through our import division at Beringer, Crosse & Blackwell Cellars. This dates back to the days when Nestlé owned Beringer and was making huge investments, bringing it back from near oblivion to new greatness and respect. In the wine business, this is like turning a battleship in the ocean. You need a lot of time and space. And friends like the Moueix family.

In France, Enjalbert was the most revered expert in wine geology. He taught at the University of Bordeaux, and his opinion in areas of geology was highly sought after from the sixties until 1983, when he passed. He was the man if you wanted an expert opinion on the potential of any winegrowing area anywhere in the world, not just France. In 1973, Nestlé hired him to travel to California and spend most of his time in Napa Valley but also assess new growing areas up and down the state.

The report, when I first saw it in 1979, was a revelation to me. No other way to describe its impact on me. His paper began with a dissertation on Thomas Jefferson's visits to Bordeaux, Languedoc, Burgundy, and the Rhineland. Jefferson stayed in Bordeaux from May 24 to 28, 1787, and his extensive observations on winegrowing and wine are safe to examine by anyone in the Library of Congress.

Following notes and quotes from Jefferson's letters, Henri moved on to George Vancouver's travels up and down the coast of California in 1792, 1793, and 1794. Vancouver made detailed notes on the geography, climates, and soils of California. As a man of the Siècle des Lumières, his observations are brilliant and detailed. He envisioned California's exceptional potential in the world of agriculture, and his astute comments hold up today.

Everything's better with some wine in the belly.

—GEORGE R. R. MARTIN
AUTHOR OF A GAME OF THRONES

Enjalbert pointed out the potential of each Napa Valley appellation and subappellation he examined, and his detailed notes and guidelines are relevant today. Beringer took advantage of this private report and used it to help contract and buy vineyards that would lay the foundation of its Private Reserve programs for Cabernet Sauvignon and Chardonnay over the following decades and expand its outreach to new appellations, winery, and vineyard purchases. To understand the geological history of Napa Valley, I recommend *The Winemaker's Dance: Exploring Terroir in the Napa Valley*, by Jonathan Swinchatt and David G. Howell. I shared a panel with one of the authors in New York, discussing the Oakville appellation and its ancient history. Great book for anyone thirsty to get down deep into the dirt of Napa.

Nestlé also hired winemaking consultants from Bordeaux to help us understand Cabernet Sauvignon in particular. I contacted importer Martine Saunier, who would later help me find a consultant from Burgundy to focus on Pinot Noir. Jean-Louis Mandrau, director of wine at Château Latour in Bordeaux from 1970 to 1983, and Patrick Léon, who had worked as winemaker at Château Mouton Rothschild, were two consultants—very smart guys to bring to the table to talk and taste and open up discussions about Cabernet Sauvignon, Cabernet Franc, Petit Verdot, and Merlot. Of the Cinq Cépages, there was little conversation about Malbec.

One conversation stayed with me longer than any other, and it was Mandrau who led it. His argument was that the Cinq Cépages varieties were originally planted in Bordeaux because they ripened on different schedules. If a vineyard was hit by frost, hail, heavy rain, or another weather event, that might wipe out one of the varieties, but the others would have a chance to make it to the finish line intact. Their collective existence was an insurance policy as much as it was varietals that complemented each other in a wine.

Mandrau went on with a postulation that Napa Valley does not have as many of the weather events in a growing season that could wipe a variety out as did Bordeaux, and we could potentially rely on one basic varietal to achieve greatness or success. This variety was Cabernet Sauvignon, which he felt was the most suited of the Cinq Cépages family for the climate and soils of Napa Valley. Fifty years later, I think his argument has been proven correct. However, a more profound point came at the end of our discussion.

Mandrau suggested that Cabernet's ability in most years to ripen in many of Napa Valley's appellations made it possible to make a complex wine out of Cabernets from different sites. In the hands of a good winemaker, the different expressions of Cabernet would make a complex and complete wine in every vintage. Such a wine would be bulletproof in an off vintage.

In hindsight, he mapped out what was to become the Beringer Private Reserve program. It started as a single vineyard program and then expanded to a wine made mostly from Cabernet from multiple vineyards. I was part of a team that helped shape the early Private Reserve Cabernets, and I watched it grow under Ed Sbragia's direction over thirty years. Ed worked hard shaping each blended Reserve, tasting hundreds of barrel samples each year to get it right. He is a gifted blender. Today, when I put his Reserves against the top wines of any vintage in Napa Valley, they stand proudly on the medal podium.

Ed, Patrick Léon, and Jean-Louis Mandrau were all huge fans of the single-vineyard Cabernets of Napa Valley. All championed these solo expressions of Cabernet during our blind tastings of other Napa Valley— and Bordeaux—producers against our wines. I felt very privileged to be invited to these tastings and watch the single-vineyard program grow under Ed's direction. Patrick would go on to make the first vintages of Opus One. A man with a sense of humor and great taste in wine, he passed one week before we were to meet again in Bordeaux in 2018.

Two Napa Valley winemakers I wish I had known better are John Kongsgaard and Tony Soter. Our paths crossed many times, Kongsgaard participated in my Master Series on Food and Wine in 2001, but I never had as many opportunities as I would like to listen to their thoughts on making and growing Cabernet and Chardonnay in Napa Valley. Tony has a sixth sense about which vineyards would make great wine. These include Vine Hill Ranch Vineyard and what is now Scarecrow. Tony moved to Oregon in 1997, but I collect the wines he made in Napa and am never disappointed.

Kongsgaard planted vineyards in the 1970s and has made legendary wines in Napa Valley since the early nineties. He has mentored many winemakers like Aaron Pott, who have in turn mentored more. John's classical live music series brought musicians from all over the world to the Napa Valley for decades, and he traveled the world to witness Wagner's *Ring* wherever it played. My favorite quote from John is, "If you have to travel to Florida to sell your wine, you're making too much wine."

Like Tony's wines, I buy and drink John's wines with pleasure, knowing his contributions. Try and find his Judge Chardonnay. Both John and Tony, without drawing attention to themselves, helped shape the Napa Valley of today. I wish I had the space here to honor all the men and women who have participated in this mentorship program. They know who they are, and please know I salute you. Thanks.

THE GREATEST TEACHER OF THEM ALL: MAKING YOUR OWN WINE AND LEARNING FROM YOUR MISTAKES

Every year from 1983 to 1996, I begged and borrowed a large flatbed truck, loaded it with fifty small lug boxes, and invited wine writers, chefs, and would-be celebrities to make wine with me. We gathered at daybreak, drove to a designated vineyard—whether Caymus (thanks to the Wagners), State Lane, Bancroft, St. Helena, Chabot, my own home vineyard (planted with David Abreu)—and picked until the boxes were full and then headed back to my small crusher-stemmer set up outside my winery office. I opened the rollers a little farther apart than normal, so we kept a lot of whole berries in the must. When the last box of grapes was crushed, I invited everyone who wanted to stomp the must to jump in, and most did. This gave the mix a good extra-gentle crush. Think Lucille Ball's episode in *I Love Lucy* (find it on YouTube) and you get the picture.

After hoisting the last box of grapes into the crusher stemmer, we hosed down all the winemakers and led them to a long harvest lunch at Beringer (Gary Danko was our chef for a good number of those years) with older wines from our vineyards. After our late lunch, everyone went home. I stayed to clean up the crush station, which usually took a few extra hours. Somehow, my memory is that the cleanup was very satisfying, especially when we had the potential for a great wine. To moderate the temperature during the next two weeks of fermentation, I used a forklift to move the fermentation bins in and out of the sun. Very high-tech.

I used winemaking's basket press, and we pressed direct to barrel and then moved them to a special corner of the cellar with other Beringer Cabernets. These "homemades" were topped regularly, racked twice, and then bottled two years later—unfiltered, unfined. Very little manipulation, minimal racking or introduction to air. One wine has died on me; the rest fill me with pride and awe. The mistakes I made along the way were mostly around picking dates—getting those right or not—and learning to taste the grapes, not solely relying on the numbers from the lab to narrow the picking window. One year, I missed topping a barrel, and it was given a proper burial. We top religiously now. When wine evaporates in a barrel or when we taste it, we need to replace it immediately. A spotlessly clean winery and well-topped barrels pave the road to good wine.

Possibly the most important attitude for a winemaker is to stay curious, to remember there are always lessons to learn, and to pay attention to all the details. The devil is in there, but so are the angels. Researching this book, I pulled out a photo without a date on it, but it was around this time of making small lots of wine in my little winery in the bigger winery. Good times. I'm in the photo surrounded by people I worked closely with, and all were the curious types—always exploring and trying new things out in their area of expertise. All worked with me at Beringer when we were pushing envelopes, exploring.

In this picture are Ed Sbragia, Bob Steinhauer, Jane Robichaux, Tim Hanni, and Jerry Comfort, all smiling at the camera, situated in and around an old Packard convertible with boxes of wine hanging out the back. We are toasting the camera with the Beringer Rhine House behind us. For over twenty years, I worked to come up with a Beringer auction item for Auction Napa Valley that we felt would compete with our peers and raise some serious dollars for education and health care in Napa Valley. This photo had to be attached to one of those auction items. It says to me, "Bid on this group of dreamers and their wines; bid high. You're going to have a whole lot of fun hanging with us."

Ed Sbragia is, of course, the winemaker. Bob Steinhauer managed all of Beringer's vineyards, along with other brands under the Beringer Wine Estates umbrella. Bob was family to us all, a bit larger than life, and one of the valley's most respected viticulturalists. Jane Robichaux was hired by Ed to manage a winery we had built within the larger winery to make experimental wines so we could speed up the learning process. Each harvest, all winemakers and wineries have usually one classroom to walk into and learn. Jane and her experimental winery afforded us other classrooms, impossible on a larger scale. I spent a lot of time with Jane, picking her brain, tasting experiments, and borrowing her basket press to press my wines.

Tim Hanni is the most entertaining and provocative wine educator I know. I hired him for his groundbreaking approach to wine education. At Beringer, we helped Tim with his run at getting a Master of Wine qualification. He became one of the first two Americans to earn that prestigious honor. Jerry Comfort was our Hudson House chef for private events. He and Tim made a great pair, and both became celebrities in that arena of wine and food educators. It was one hell of a team to work with, and we all put in long days and sometimes—no, many times—long nights. I would do it all over again. I learned a lot from all of them. Every one of them stayed curious all the years we worked together.

The year 2001 was my last at Beringer. The company was large, complex, and had a new owner and direction. It was changing again, as all corporations do, and Ed and Bob were the final two standing of our original executive committee. I was retiring with a full final year to create a new wine and food program and mentor.

The program I developed was called the Masters Series on Food and Wine. I was its founder, and its shape and purpose were simple and inclusive. We invited world-class chefs to cook and world-class wineries to work with us to share their wines with lucky patrons who paid for the privilege of sharing the experiences we put together. Five days of food and wine heaven. The chefs included Julia Child, Thomas Keller, Madeleine Kamman, Gary Danko, Cindy Pawlcyn, Bradley Ogden, Hiro Sone, and others. Some of the wineries I asked to share their cellars and kitchens were Spottswoode, Staglin, Far Niente, Kongsgaard, Stag's Leap Wine Cellars, Viader, Long Meadow Ranch, David Arthur, Barnett, Amizetta, and others. No one said no to my request to join the party, and we did party and made a lot of friends.

The key element of the Master Series was a shared community. We promoted Napa Valley, its wines, its people, its restaurants, hotels, and its greatest strength of all: its collective willingness to work together for a greater whole. Sounds too simple. Pollyannaish. But it was and still is at the core of Napa Valley's extraordinary success story the decades I have worked in this small valley of dreamers. It is also its future. Andy Beckstoffer again demanded I have villains in this book. The villains here are those, who, for self-interests, tear at this core, develop their own silos, monuments mostly to themselves, and foster an environment that darkens the waters around them. Here, they are but a minority. If this minority grows and builds more silos, others will follow, and soon that will be the landscape. I'm the optimist, but we do need to stay vigilant.

Bacchus opens up the gates of the heart.

—**HORACE**
ITALIAN POET AND PHILOSOPHER, 65–8 BCE

DECEMBER

THE YEAR HAS BEEN A BLUR. Happens when you are always in motion, most of that forward and most of that out of your control. Mother Nature guides our paths in winemaking, and our lives revolve around her. The last decade in Napa Valley is a very stark reminder of who runs the show. I don't think having a winery and wearing many hats works well for control freaks. Mother Nature will slap you down until you change, never the other way around. Humility is often rewarded, but not all the time. Just enough, however, to keep some egos in check.

The Napa Valley wine community is about relationships. When I started TOR, I was not convinced, but I am now. Relationships are the engine. Without them, I would not have access to the grapes I do. I would not have the earned respect of the growers, my customers, or the trade and media.

In December, friends and family visit to celebrate and honor these relationships maybe more than in other months. Some of these important relationships did not come easy, but once tested a few times, they were strengthened.

In the winery, it is time for cleaning up the equipment and putting it away for the following year. Some fermentations are still ticking. Most of these are the second fermentation we call malolactic fermentation—converting those two acids, softening the wine, and building another layer of flavors. The microflora, or yeasts, that perform this miracle come in from the vineyard, but like the primary fermentation, they can be added. It is a winemaker's choice. It will influence the flavor and character of the wine significantly.

In the vineyard, we are cleaning up, possibly beginning the pruning cycle, and mending fences. December is typically cold and damp. I spent

WHAT DO THEY ADD TO A WINE?

Wine is natural all on its own and defines "natural" if you pay attention to who is making it. The best wines do not need additions other than a minuscule touch of sulfur dioxide measured in parts per million. This SO$_2$ also occurs naturally in every wine. Those who may have a problem with SO$_2$ at these levels are also measured in parts per million. Wine has saved armies and built civilizations because it was safer than the water.

a good deal of my youth in Southern California and did not know winter. Napa Valley introduced me to winter, and I love it. A winter chill and misty fog drift through the vineyards as you walk alongside the vines with your dog and your friends. The bigger wines taste better, the food is bolder, the expectations for the next year are high.

This is a month to be appreciative, to reflect on the relationships that got you where you are today. And it's a wonderful month for romance—but then, hopefully, they all are.

RELATIONSHIPS AND ROMANCE

MYRON AND ALICE The Nightingales were one of the happiest couples I've ever met. They did everything together, and Myron was at his best and funniest when his redhead was near. Myron was the first winemaker I ever worked with. He was Beringer's winemaker in the seventies and was enlisted with the task of turning the old winery around. He was a quiet winemaking legend in the seventies and eighties—everyone in the business knew Myron, and most knew Alice. She pioneered the first botrytised sweet wines in California in the fifties with Myron's help.

Myron's first day at Beringer in 1971 was almost his last. He was escorted into the stately Rhine House, one of Napa Valley's most beautiful mansions, built for Frederick Beringer in 1883 during the early golden age. There, in a back room of the mansion, his winemaker's office and laboratory consisted of a table mounted on two sawhorses and a chair. He blinked a few times and turned around to leave, but he was coaxed back, and stayed for the rest of his life. This is the story he told me.

When Myron and I boarded our first plane to the East Coast for a series of seminars and tastings in 1978, he had been making wine in California for close to four decades. He had worked wineries in Lodi, Asti, and Livermore before finally settling in Napa Valley, a dream come true for Alice and him. His new boss was Nestlé of Switzerland—his immediate boss was Dick Maher, president of Beringer during my first years. When Myron was away from the winery on business trips, he expected me to be in charge of setting up tastings, dinners, lunches, and travel schedules.

Myron was about five feet, three inches; medium build; bald; and wore workingman's glasses. When at work, he dressed in slacks and short-sleeved dress shirts. Now that I think about it, he dressed that way at home, too. All of that contributed to a first impression of him as an organized, serious man, but this was deceiving. He could be very mischievous. He had a wonderful and sometimes inappropriate sense of humor. Occasionally, it was my job to edit this, but for those of us who spent a lot of time with Myron, we would often be brought to tears by comments that escaped. Zingers.

Alice was a more imposing figure than Myron. She was possibly taller, certainly heavier, and she let her opinions be known immediately and often loudly. You always knew if she was on your side or not—and *not* was not a good country to visit. Alice suffered no fools and fiercely protected Myron if she felt he was not getting the credit and attention he deserved. Myron, on the other hand, was less forthcoming about his true opinions, soft-spoken, self-deprecating—and did I mention the zingers? After dinner one night, when Alice had momentarily left the table, Myron explained the reason for his baldness: "Too many U-turns under the sheets." They made a formidable team of opposites, hopelessly attracted to each other for reasons only the heart knows.

When I was hired by Beringer in 1977, lunches for visiting dignitaries were cold cuts, bread, salads, and accoutrements from Giugni's, a local deli. Later, I would oversee Beringer's culinary direction. We hired chefs like Gary Danko, who stayed with me for six years, and eventually built the Hudson House kitchen and hospitality building, a true culinary center, home to cooking schools and many celebrity chefs. But in those early days, it was cold cuts and sides. Myron aptly described this fare as "donkey dick and potato salad." I warned you—zingers that flew in strange directions at any time.

From 1971 to 1987, Myron did what a lot of veteran winemakers thought impossible: he tore down the old winery, cleaned everything up, built a new one, and then expanded. His first lab, the basic chemistry-test equipment balanced on sawhorses in the Rhine House, evolved into a modern winery across the street, with its own large formal lab, where important tests could be done. Plus, he had full-time winemaking and lab assistants who admired him.

In the late seventies and early eighties, part of my job was to get Myron on the road and to work with winemakers on defining new wines that could ultimately compete with Napa Valley's best. The two most popular wines when I started at Beringer were Barenblut and Traubengold. The former was a red blend whose name translates to "blood of the bear." I never learned what went into that wine; it was not memorable. Traubengold was a semisweet Riesling made from Santa Maria grapes grown near the Central California coast. The third most popular wine was a cream sherry—it made a killer sherry cake that my mother loved.

A year later, we were working on rapid changes. We began a new Private Reserve program for Chardonnay and Cabernet and started barrel-fermented Chardonnay—most California Chardonnay at the time was fermented in steel and barrel aged. Myron was not a fan of oak barrels and wine—he preferred clean-tasting wines without the influences of oak—but he was game. His favorite beverage, by a good measure, was his "English Chablis"—Beefeater with a twist. Alice's favorite was Tanqueray, also with a twist. When we boarded a flight together, no matter what time of day, Myron and Alice would have two of each from the first pass of the beverage cart.

Being young and wanting to pack the travel week with as much as I could, I made a near-fatal mistake one year. I scheduled a brutal four-city trip and told Myron that we would have to do this one by ourselves—no Alice. I was truly concerned for her health. Alice was less mobile than Myron and sometimes used a wheelchair in airports. Immediately, I was put in the Nightingale doghouse, and on our return, I was not invited to our regular dinners out as friends. I had crossed the line. Myron and Alice traveled together whenever possible. End of story, as they say.

The situation worsened no matter what overtures I made. Alice was again part of our Flying Circus, but she was cold and frankly let it be known that she did not enjoy my company one bit. I needed to do something big to get back into the redhead's good graces. By then, I was writing all the winemaker comments on vintages, winemaking, and viticulture for the marketing materials, and I knew everything about the Nightingales' past, including their large contributions to winemaking from the forties up to their move to Napa.

Their famous Premier Sémillon, made at Cresta Blanca Winery in Livermore in the fifties, was groundbreaking. It was California's very first botrytised wine, made sweet to mimic the great Sauternes from France. These wines, as Myron informed me, were really Alice's project. Her children had married and left the house, and Alice needed something to fill the gaps. With help from UC Davis and some of its best winemaking minds, Myron and Alice began Premier Sémillon, a wine truly ahead of its time. Alice loved the project and became the driving force behind it.

Myron and Tor, with Myron thinking, "What is that wine snob doing?"

Botrytised sweet white wines are among the world's most collectible. They can age a century under rare conditions and for decades under normal ones. They are honeyed, sweet, unbelievably complex wines, and at their best worthy of all the prestige. However, they rely on a much-prescribed set of weather conditions that are not as common in most parts of California as they are in Sauternes, Barsac, or parts of Germany and Hungary. So, Alice isolated the botrytis spores—yes, botrytis is a fungus—as the English termed it, a noble rot—and then propagated them. With the help of Myron and her comrades at UC Davis, Alice also created a closed environment where they could control the weather conditions, laid the grapes out on custom-made trays, and sprayed them with the isolated *Botrytis cinerea* spores.

They made amazing wines with this somewhat complicated process. One day, while I was talking to Myron, a dim light of inspiration pointed a way out of Alice's doghouse. I set up a meeting with Jim Tonjum, vice president of Beringer and my boss, and explained why it was so important to begin the process of making these wines at Beringer again. There was a great story—the pioneers were back together making botrytised wines. Other winemakers, like Dick Arrowood and Joseph Phelps, were making botrytised Rieslings, and others were following. Nothing was impossible for California's new wave of winemakers. We were shooting for the stars. Beringer wanted to be a player.

Though it would be a considerable expense setting everything up for Alice to take over, Jim and Dick Maher agreed to finance the project. The last step was to meet with Myron and Alice together and ask them if they would consider making another great botrytised Sémillon using their methods from Cresta Blanca. Alice was stunned, or very thoughtful, or both. She said she would think about it and left the room. Myron said nothing but winked at me. Alice was about to welcome the lost son back into the family. And Beringer was about to have a very special new wine.

Launching "Nightingale" wine at the Biltmore Hotel in Los Angeles, 1984: (left to right) Chef Roland Gilbert, Tor, Alice, GM Bernard Jacoupy, and Myron

In 1980, Alice made her first botrytised Sémillon at Beringer. By then Alice, Myron, and I were back together going out to dinner. I stuck to wine, and they always started the meal with a little of that English Chablis. I was out of the doghouse.

When Jim asked what we should call the wine, I believe my answer was quick—Nightingale. We could have called it Sweet Alice, but Nightingale set the perfect tone and right pitch. What a delightful couple. Occasionally, the press would get to them without a filter. In *Wine Spectator* one year, Myron was asked about the vintage and said relatively complimentary things, except when he remarked, "Chenin Blanc sure took it in the shorts."

Sometimes, I just miss them. In many ways, they define a lost period of Napa's history. One we can't go back to again. Myron's dad worked the railroads. They were children of low-income families, had survived world wars and the Great Depression. Winemaking was a job, and the terms *passion*, *art*, and *the good life* were not a part of his vocabulary. It was just another way to make a living. Napa was known for its mental institution more than its wines when Myron and Alice entered the scene. A few martinis, a good steak, baked potato, and salad was a great meal out. One earned through hard work and determination.

Myron and Alice have both passed. There is a plaque at the Culinary Institute of America (CIA) in Napa Valley acknowledging Myron as one of Napa Valley's legends. His verbal history was recorded for UC Berkeley's Bancroft Library and is in print form at the St. Helena Public Library, in case anyone wants to read more about the humble but great man. Or, if you visit me, ask to see one of the copies in my wine library.

Myron and Alice are best remembered through Beringer's Nightingale wines. They have aged beautifully. The first 1980 vintage has vibrancy and complexity and gives pleasure. It is a bit more golden than it was in 1983 when it was released. But then, so are my memories of Myron and Alice.

SUSAN AND TOR I was thirty-eight years old when I met Susan Costner. I was happily unmarried—possibly married to my business—and getting to the age where I was untrainable to be a soulmate for anything but the life of a roving vintner. I was set in my ways, and so was Susan. Strangely, we still are today—strong-minded—but it works in many wonderful ways.

Susan came to Napa Valley for the first time with a celebrity status as a taste master and food writer. She had written two cookbooks and was working on her third with Crown Publishing Group. She was a huge celebrity in the Hamptons in New York, where she and her friend Devon Fredericks had started a takeout and catering business they called Loaves

Susan Costner promotional picture
and a couple of her cookbooks

and Fishes. Over the years, Susan has told me stories of all the celebrities, artists, musicians, and regulars who frequented the store and who she catered for. They would trade catering services for local but famous artists' work, and Susan became close friends with the internationally acclaimed dual pianists Bobby Fizdale and Arthur Gold, who were also the food editors of *Vogue*. She and Devon were in their twenties, and the memories were indelible, bright, and very exciting for the enterprising young women.

In 1985, the year we met, Susan took a job with *Working Woman* magazine and hitched a ride to the West Coast to work on a story about women in the wine business. She had no plans to stay, but she liked the idea of finishing the next cookbook and the article on women winemakers in Napa Valley. It was a happening scene.

Stu Smith was chair that year of the Napa Valley Wine Auction, our biggest fundraiser and show-off event of the year. Susan, his wife, introduced us at a dinner party. Susan Costner—that was her maiden name—was one of the most beautiful women I had ever seen. I know this is trite, but she was. She was also funny and intelligent and had a fabulous laugh. She was comfortable in her own skin, and beneath the skin was a woman you sensed loved life, people, and adventure. She asked me if she could visit me at the winery and apply for a job. I might have been a little nervous. "Sure," was my stupid reply, and we set a date.

I did not have a job for her, and HR would have admonished me if they had found out that I had implied that I did, but we discussed wine and food and our favorite chefs for some time. Gary Danko, our Beringer chef at the time, remembers walking into my office during her visit—in his words, "The sparks were flying." Again, I did not have a job, full- or part-time, for her skill set. If I had been smart, I would have made one up, but I didn't. This would happen later, and she still complains she was not compensated for all the brilliant work she did for Beringer over the years we worked together as husband and wife. Very fair complaint. Very.

After a long conversation, interrupted by Gary, I said, "Susan, I don't have a job for you right now, but would you be interested in a date?" HR would have fired me on the spot. Before she could say no, I elaborated: "It would be at the home of Belle and Barney Rhodes, who would love to introduce you to a wide range of women winemakers, chefs, and the inner world of Napa Valley movers and shakers. They're wonderful people, have invited me for dinner this week, and I'm fairly sure they would love to meet you."

She said, "Yes." She tells the story that I gave her a tour of the Beringer caves afterward—and that I gave off some kind of heat, or something. I really don't remember this. I must have been a little numb and very happy with her "Yes." Maybe I did give a private tour that day.

At Belle and Barney's dinner parlor, she was an instant celebrity. They had her two cookbooks in their extensive food and wine library (which they would later donate to the CIA), knew all about Loaves and Fishes, and made her feel Napa Valley had potential for the months she might stay and finish her work. I flew out early the next morning on a business trip to Hawaii—I was presenting a seminar on food and wine at a symposium on the Big Island. I called her the first night, saying how much I'd enjoyed our time together. What I didn't say was that I wished she was in Hawaii with me.

Our courtship was fast and, though maybe not furious, exhilarating. I proposed to her the following year at the French Laundry. 1986. It was a very good vintage in Napa Valley. Our wedding was in our backyard—close friends and family only. The wedding dinner inside the Beringer Rhine House with Gary Danko as chef. The toasts were as good as the food, and the wine included six bottles of 1959 Domaine de la Romanée-Conti. We drove to Campton Place in San Francisco for a very short night, then on to Paris early the next day for our honeymoon. We've been running all over the world since, maybe trying to keep this honeymoon alive. Two brilliant and very independent children have not slowed us down. They've followed their dreams, and we are immensely proud of both of them. I brag about their moral compasses—different but both dedicated to helping other people live better lives. So proud.

Susan has supported me in so many ways, it would take another book to fully explain just how, and we've made a good team. She wrote three more cookbooks: *Good Friends, Great Dinners*, which includes photos of our first child, Molly, and our circle of friends at the time; *Susan Costner's Great Sandwiches*, which won the prestigious James Beard Award for best book in its category; and *Mostly Vegetables*, a book ahead of its time. All three are relevant today. Our friends, as well as Susan and I, still cook from them. Susan also signed me up for a weekly column we wrote together for *Parenting* called Food and Whine. It was a bit corny, but we had fun talking about raising children and enjoying a little wine and food together.

For Beringer, she wrote a series of food and wine magazines that had a devoted following called *Tables*. She also assisted me with many wine and food extravaganzas at Beringer and on the road. These included a yearlong celebration of American regional cuisines, Japanese and other Asian cuisines, and wine, but the most memorable and possibly notable was our yearlong series on great female chefs.

The idea for Great Women Chefs was not mine—it was all Susan's, and the timing was perfect. In the seventies and eighties, I think it's fair to say

Susan Kenward: wife, mother, cookbook author, and vintner

that female restaurant chefs were not given the same opportunities as their male counterparts. The same with recognition—it was not a level playing field. Madeleine Kamman, who had joined us at Beringer to educate and train young chefs, was very adamant about this and a bit resentful. With Susan's guidance, in 1987, we invited famous female chefs from all over the country to stay for a year to cook and teach.

The culminating event celebrating female chefs was a huge benefit for the American Institute of Wine & Food. Julia Child, who had asked me to join its board, was hugely supportive of Susan's yearlong focus on female chefs. We sold out immediately—or oversold it. I forget how many hundreds attended, filling every inch of the Beringer grounds. It was a culinary and social event reported in *Town & Country*, society pages, and all the national

---

THE MENU

Domaine Chandon Reserve

1983 Iron Horse Vineyards Blanc de Blancs
Sonoma County Green Valley

1982 Schramsberg Blanc de Noir

·

BARBARA TROPP
China Moon — Crispy Spring Rolls Stuffed with Curried Chicken, Glass Noodles & Toasted Peanuts with Fresh Chili Dipping Sauce

·

Confetti Shao-Mai Dumplings with Fresh Water Chestnuts

·

MARGARET FOX
Cafe Beaujolais — Home Smoked Salmon with Fresh Dill & Mascarpone Cheese on a Canape

·

MARY SUE MILLIKEN
The City Restaurant — Corn Tamales with Sour Cream & Salsa / Sweet Roasted Peppers with Feta Cheese

·

AMY FERGUSON
Baby Routh — Wok-Charred Tuna with Ginger Tomatillo Sauce Garnished with Sunflower Sprouts & Julienne of Daikon & Carrot

1985 Cain Cellars Carneros Chardonnay

1986 Cakebread Cellars Sauvignon Blanc

1985 Domaine Michel Chardonnay

1985 Monticello Chevrier Blanc

1986 Simi Rose of Cabernet

·

JOYCE GOLDSTEIN
Square One and Caffe Quadro — Chilled Gazpacho with Prawns

1984 Freemark Abbey Chardonnay

1985 Trefethen White Riesling

·

MARY SUE MILLIKEN
The City Restaurant — Lop Cheung Salad with Cucumbers, Scallions & Serranos

·

LESLEE REIS
Cafe Provencal — Pan Browned Garlic Sausages with Herbed Potato Salad & Fresh Tomato Relish

·

LYDIA SHIRE
Four Seasons Hotel — Grilled Lobster & Bluefish with Crisp Summer Beans

1983 Inglenook Napa Valley Charbono

1980 Joseph Phelps Alexander Valley Zinfandel

1984 Sterling Merlot

Grilled Chipotle Quail, Wild Rice Pumpkin Seed Salad & Mango-Tomato Salsa — **AMY FERGUSON** *Baby Routh*

·

Herb Cured Pork Loins with Fresh Fruit Chutney & Fresh Herb Riot — **CYNTHIA PAWLCYN** *Mustards Grill and Fog City Diner*

·

Grilled Summer Sweet Corn with Lime Chili Butter — **JOYCE GOLDSTEIN** *Square One and Caffe Quadro*

·

Grilled Market Vegetables with Aillade — **ANNIE SOMERVILLE** *Greens*

1984 Acacia Iund Pinot Noir

1982 Beringer Private Reserve Cabernet Sauvignon

1983 Far Niente Cabernet Sauvignon

·

Herbed Rosemary Bread — **JOYCE GOLDSTEIN** *Square One and Caffe Quadro*

·

Sourdough Bagettes, Walnut Bread, Pain de Campagne — **KAREN MITCHELL** *Model Bakery*

·

Mixed Greens Salad with a Lemon Tarragon Vinaigrette & Assorted Cheeses from Laura Chenel — **ANNIE SOMERVILLE** *Greens*

1981 Jordan Cabernet Sauvignon

1983 Sebastiani Zinfandel

·

Assorted Berry Sorbets with Fresh Summer Fruits — **LINDSEY SHERE & ALICE WATERS** *Chez Panisse*

China Moon's Cookies of Good Fortune — **BARBARA TROPP** *China Moon*

·

Warm Berries & Peaches with Shortcake Biscuits & Whipped Cream — **MARGARET FOX** *Cafe Beaujolais*

·

Bitter Sweet Chocolate Pecan Torte with Homemade Raspberry Jam & Chocolate Glaze — **LESLEE REIS** *Cafe Provencal*

1983 Robert Mondavi Botrytised Sauvignon Blanc

The Christian Brothers' 1980 Napa Valley Zinfandel Port

Great Women Chefs menus

culinary publications. If you were a serious foodie, that was one of the top ten tickets for the year on the West Coast, possibly in all the United States.

The person in charge of logistics, making sure all the temporary kitchens for the chefs worked, was a man, Gary Danko, who busted his butt to make it all happen. I can't describe his hard work any differently. Beringer had no large central kitchen, and each chef had to work from a makeshift kitchen using propane or fire, refrigeration, and preprepared dishes. It was a monumental task with a lot of working parts. Without Gary literally putting out fires and building them, it would have been a different night. But the show went on, all the dishes were excellent, chefs and attendees exuberant.

On center stage was the brilliance of women in America, and their contributions to a true culinary revolution in America at the time. The chefs— Alice Waters (Chez Panisse and Café Fanny, Berkeley), Barbara Tropp (China Moon, San Francisco), Lydia Shire (Four Seasons, Los Angeles), Joyce Goldstein (Square One, San Francisco), Amy Ferguson (Baby Routh, Dallas), Mary Sue Milliken and Susan Feniger (City Restaurant and Border Grill, Los Angeles), Margaret Fox (Café Beaujolais, Mendocino), Cindy Pawlcyn (Mustards Grill, Napa, and Fog City Diner, San Francisco), Lindsey Shere (Chez Panisse, Berkeley), Anne Rosenzweig (Arcadia and 21 Club, New York) and Annie Somerville (Greens, San Francisco). Julia Child was there, as were many of America's great male chefs—and Madeleine, of course.

Madeleine and Julia were not the best of friends, to say the least, but differences were put aside that night. We invited twenty-one neighboring wineries to pour and join in the celebration. One of our dear friends, Gary Wagner, handled the decorations. The volunteer efforts from supporting chefs, wineries, and wine and food aficionados were huge. Gary Danko was still shutting down food stations when the morning light started a new day. We were all tired but elated—there was a lot of good juju in the air. Proud night for all.

Afterward, Madeleine explained a well-formed opinion that women cook heartier food than men. They cook on a larger, bolder scale than men, she argued, especially when you get to the top tiers in their profession. She would list several three-star Michelin chefs we both knew, and I would have a very hard time putting up much of an argument in some cases. A lot of great male chefs have more of a calculated touch and feel to their craft.

I reflected on some of the great three-star meals I had in France in my early travels. Restaurant Jamin in Paris, Alain Chapel in the French countryside, Marc Meneau's L'Espérance in Vézelay, Pierre Gagnaire in Saint-Étienne and in Paris. Pierre Gagnaire in Saint-Étienne was my most memorable of all the three-star experiences. His menu degustation played on every corner of my palate like a full orchestration, hitting all the right notes like a fugue building

Chef Gary Danko and cookbook author Anne Lindsay Greer with Tor in front of Beringer's Rhine House during early years of Napa Valley's culinary revolution.

note on note, making true music. No missteps—every dish connected to the one before and the one after. It was pure genius. This did not happen often, but when it did, , it created a lifetime special memory.

The women Madeleine championed cooked with great technique, big flavors, and soul. Their talents were on display that night. It was not three-star food. It was food cooked on grills with everything fresh and in season, more Californian than French, and perfect for that night, that time, that place.

Later, Julia Child would often call if there was an open seat at her table when she was in the valley. One day, she called and invited Susan and me to the French Laundry with Bob and Margrit Mondavi. Susan, though a great cookbook author and foodie, declined because she was not in the mood for the five-hour Thomas Keller experience that night. I went alone but understood her decision. Susan has rarely gravitated to this type of dining experience. She cooks brilliantly day in and day out at home, creating meals I fondly remember sharing with friends, along with good wines. Her flavors are bigger, as Madeleine has suggested. Thomas Keller is a genius, but Susan has prepared the greatest meals in my life, and no one else comes close. Her meals pair well with our wines—the flavors are always clear, true, and honest. Like the chef—who I dedicate this book to.

I'm a lucky guy. Luck be my lady tonight.

THE PERFECT WINE AND FOOD EXPERIENCE

In 1983, I was invited by the president of CVNE—Compañía Vinícola del Norte de España, one of Spain's most revered wineries in La Rioja—to visit the winery and spend three days with him. I was vice president of a company that imported the brand at the time to the United States, and this was my first trip to Spain.

Luis Vallejo Chalbaud picked me up at the airport and became the perfect host immediately with his quiet charm and gentle manner. In my dictionary, the definition of *gentleman* is Luis. Over the course of the time I spent with him, I felt I had been invited into his family and introduced to the real Spain—rich in history, culture, food, and wine. All morning and

WHAT SCORE DID ROBERT PARKER GIVE THIS WINE?
Google it. Robert once told me his score was his opinion on one wine at one moment in time. It can change. Your opinion should never be discounted against anyone else's. Never.

Wine improves with age—I like it more the older I get.

—ANONYMOUS

early afternoon, we toured the vineyards and wineries, then ate lunch at 3 or 4 P.M. for several hours, then on to famous cities, churches, and shrines late in the afternoon. We finished the day with a lighter meal around 9 or 10 P.M.

The last day of my visit, he asked me what I wanted to do and gave me some options. One was a visit to San Sebastián, a seaside town in the north known for its naval history and restaurants. One of those was a three-star Michelin called Arzak. Luis knew the chef personally and asked if I might enjoy lunch at this famous restaurant. To me, there was only one option.

It was a long drive, and we talked about the wines of La Rioja, the grape varieties, how they were grown, and the diversity of the region. Tempranillo thrived in the north, Grenache in the warmer south. CVNE was an innovator in many ways but held tradition in esteem. Luis added vivid color to much of what I'd seen the last several days, and my respect for the wines and the man grew.

When we arrived in San Sebastián, he gave me a brief tour—even today, it is one of my favorite seaside ports in the world. Next was a tour of the marketplace, overflowing with fresh seafood caught that morning, not far from the port. I had never seen many of the fish before, and I wanted to know the names, their flavors, and textures. He mentally recorded the fish I was curious about and guided me to the restaurant. It was 3 P.M.—time for lunch.

The chef, Juan Mari Arzak, came out and the two talked cordially for a while before Luis removed one wine from his satchel, a 1959 CVNE Imperial, the winery's flagship wine, made from Tempranillo. "We are going to have many courses, most of them from the seafood you showed interest in at the marketplace. The chef is going to cook just for us. All seafood. Okay?"

Okay. I had goosebumps but was curious about the wine choice. I was sure we would order a white wine for most of the fish, maybe save one meat dish for the Imperial. But I was wrong. We had the very old, aged Rioja with all the courses. Each course worked brilliantly with the wine—none seemed out of place.

Well-made, aged Tempranillo is like a fine old red Burgundy—no hard edges, layers of flavor, soft texture. All the dishes had sauces that did not interfere with, only enhanced, the wine's gentle, exquisite flavors. Though the different seafood courses had different textures and flavors, the sauces tied them to the wine, the wine to the seafood. Nothing seemed out of place. Perfection.

Perfection because of the time and place and the company at the table. Perfection because of all the backstories leading up to the meal. Perfection because of the adventure factor, new foods, and a masterful chef catering to my love of fresh seafood. Perfection because the wine had come from the personal cellar of a new friend. It was a three-and-a-half-hour food-and-wine magic show.

I learned a lot that day. The history of a rich and proud culture. The ability of a master chef to make time disappear. The secret to wine-and-food pairing—throw out the rules, except for one simple one: balance flavor, texture, and power to the wine. Simple—but, like many things, simple and pure, elusive. When you do find it, it is beautiful and most memorable.

WINE-AND-FOOD PAIRING MADE SIMPLE

Seeking perfection is dangerous because it is so elusive, or just plain subjective. What makes the perfect pairing? If it is a young red or white wine, it is fairly simple—foods that have fat, salt, and acidity that doesn't rip your face off. Find the balance in these simple ingredients. The rest are trappings, notes to add to your symphony. Avoid super-duper hot peppers or other high-heat foods, very little or no sugar, and you will enjoy world-class wine and food pairings.

Young Cabernets are fond of meats with good fat and proper salt. Young whites are the same, but you can tone it down a bit. Fish, red meat, white meat, and vegetables are the same. Find some salt and butter or good oils, play with them, and you're rounding third, headed home.

Forget the color of your wine and your food. Most people are afraid to go color-blind with their wine pairings, but you can, and quite comfortably, if you play with the salt, fat, and acids. Find the balance. If you throw most rules out the window, you'll enjoy a wider range of wines and cuisines.

It is easier than you think.

Wine makes daily living easier, less hurried, with fewer tensions and more tolerance.

—BENJAMIN FRANKLIN
AMERICAN AUTHOR, SCIENTIST, AND DIPLOMAT; 1706–1790

THE FUTURE OF NAPA VALLEY: DÉJÀ VU—THE FIFTH SEASON

AFTER THE DEVASTATING TUBBS FIRE in 2017, wherever I traveled to discuss and share wine, the first or second question was, "What about the fires? Did you have any damage?" Over the years, I've groomed my response, and it goes something like this:

In the mid-seventies, when I came to Napa Valley, there were fewer than fifty wineries, and literally everyone knew everyone who worked in the wine industry. We had no destination restaurants, hotels, or places to spend time in once the sun set unless you lived here. We were farmers first, mostly a blue-collar class of dreamers, and we got into trouble constantly trying to figure things out, so we stuck close together looking after each other. Your neighbor was family, and you needed strong bonds when Mother Nature threw unexpected punches and threw you to the ground. We had floods, cold and rainy harvests, earthquakes, phylloxera, plant viruses and their vectors, and tractors that would break down when you needed them most.

The valley changed dramatically over the decades that followed the sleepy seventies, and I've watched all this with a blend of sadness, awe, and pride. We now have over eleven hundred wine brands and eight hundred physical wineries. Billionaires discovered they could become millionaires by investing in winemaking. I watched neighbors fight over water and all the necessary permits to build and to host tourists. Some people lost sight of the prize— we live and die as an agricultural community, not as a tourist attraction. Others held on tightly. I've helped raise a family in this paradise and made more friends than I could ever imagine because of wine. I hope future generations can say the same.

The recent devastating fires of 2017 and 2020 have changed Napa Valley dramatically, in ways not seen by most visitors. I watched neighbors quickly unite and protect each other from harm. The displaced were found homes. The broken were nurtured back to health and stability. The money needed to rebuild came quickly and without strings. There were heroes everywhere as we fought back from the destruction and impact the fires had on our communities. But Napa Valley proved she was strong. A new sense of community, and of having each other's back, emerged from the ash. The fires broke our hearts—but united them.

The Fifth Season—or just plain Fire Season—brought out stories that illustrate the silver lining I'm casting on our new reality. One of my favorites has so much nuance, it's worth telling again: Let me introduce you to Lily and Jon Berlin.

Lily and Jon own El Molino Winery, which sits in the middle of Napa Valley at the base of Spring Mountain. I knew Lily's parents when they ran the winery. As the family friendship continues, Lily and Jon watch over our crazy but beautiful cocker spaniel, LuLu, when we travel. They also try to train her to be a good dog, but that is another story. Jon and Lily, like her parents, make just enough excellent Chardonnay and Pinot Noir to keep their fans happy. It is a bit of an oasis in a valley known for its Cabernet family.

El Molino was founded by Lieutenant Colonel William W. Lyman in 1871, and it is one of the oldest wineries in Napa Valley. It is the site of the very first vineyard in Napa Valley, planted to Mission grapes in 1848. A whole lot of Napa Valley history is tied up in this small winery, which sits next to the famous Bale Grist Mill, now a state historic park. For decades during the 1800s, the mill was the social center of Napa Valley.

The Glass Fire, which started on September 27, 2020, erupted violently on a hot, windy morning and spread almost as fast as light from the eastern hills to the valley floor before the sun rose. Jon looked out his window at 3:30 A.M. and witnessed exploding power lines and huge balls of fire headed his way. The mass evacuations had begun, the roads were clogging, and CAL FIRE was quickly overwhelmed. The horror and dread Jon and Lily felt were overwhelming, but they could not leave the historic winery. They would fight.

Jon was born and raised in South Africa, served in the military as a firefighter, loved surfing and winemaking, and followed his dreams to Napa Valley to be a winemaker. He is also a biker. His bike of choice is the Vertigo Trials motorcycle, a "weird" machine not well known to the outside world but with cult status among two-wheel aficionados. This trails bike is all about going slow and staying balanced as the pilot maneuvers over challenging terrain. It's the perfect mountain bike for an obsessive, fit, and excellent athlete like Jon.

Napa Valley closed down as fast as the sun rose that day. All vital arteries near its center were blocked. CAL FIRE could not keep up with fires erupting everywhere as high winds hurtled hot embers for miles in every direction. Downed trees and burned-out vehicles made it impossible to get fire trucks to homes, wineries, and people. But Jon knew the hilly terrain as well as the blocked roads and took off to fight fire. Over the following weeks, he became a legend, a hero, a savior for many of his neighbors who had no idea if their homes or wineries were still standing.

Since Jon was unable to communicate with all the people who needed vital information, Lily at the winery was his vital contact. "As word grew," Lily recalls, "people wanted his number, and I had to be the command center, as he was always on the bike for firefighting, or resting. But he always took my call or text and would go and check someone's home or winery. At one point, he ran out of food, and I had to borrow an Ag Pass [a card authorizing the bearer to access evacuation zones], as mine wasn't approved yet, and bring him supplies. He was without power and water but had a small generator going to keep his phone charged and one lamp going."

CAL FIRE battalion chief Darren Johnson became a regular contact when he realized Jon could get where he couldn't, and at one point he gave Jon his phone and told him to report. Fire often whipped on both sides as Jon rode up and down Spring Mountain with a "rinky-dink" fire-retardant pack strapped to his back. Other volunteer firefighters, like vintner/grower David Abreu, and crews worked with Jon to cut fire lines. These, without doubt, saved homes and wineries. Jon, as he will tell you, is only one of hundreds of professionals and volunteers who put their lives on the line to help others while the fire raged on for days. They are all our neighbors and friends. They are part of our past, our present, and our future.

This is the story I tell. These stories are part of us, but so is the spirit that fires will not define us. That is what our wine will do. This story has drama and nuance. Lily and Jon chose to stay and fight for the survival of their winery and their neighbors' homes. They are a new generation of winemakers, two generations separated from Robert Mondavi and Andre Tchelistcheff, my mentors. Their winery is one of Napa's cherished wineries, dating back to its earliest winemaking history. Their only red wine is Pinot Noir, which makes them renegades in a world of Cabernet Sauvignon. We had renegades, when I came to Napa in the seventies, making Petite Sirah,

Riesling, Charbono, and dozens of other varieties that were exceptional, but theirs became the road less traveled with time. We need renegades in every generation. We need diversity.

The Cabernet family will reign for my lifetime. I also feel, without hesitation, that many of Napa Valley's greatest wines are ahead of us. The 2018 and 2019 vintages are proof that the wines are better than ever. We are making huge investments in firefighting technology and equipment and in how to adjust to climate change. My neighbors are survivors, fighters, and lovers. That is why I live in the middle of Napa Valley.

A PARTING TOAST TO YOUR HEALTH

As long as there's been written history of humankind, wine has been linked to good health and praised for its benefits. I'm an advocate of everyone finding their own way of bringing wine into their lives. It is not for everyone, but what is life, except for oxygen, water, and a little love? I disagree with anyone who tells me that each glass of wine I enjoy limits my health and my life span. Julia Child told me she would much rather enjoy her glass of wine or a cocktail each day than live the extra days the absence might add: "Not worth it, in my book." (But she lived to be almost ninety-two anyway.)

The person known to have lived the longest died when she was 122 years and 164 days old. Jeanne Calment resided in the South of France, enjoyed cycling and roller-skating, and had a very good sense of humor: "I've never had but one wrinkle, and I'm sitting on it." She was optimistic and well liked in her community—and enjoyed wine most every day. Enjoying the life that we live might have a lot to do with our health. It seemed to work for Jeanne. If longevity is our goal, maybe we should take up roller-skating. Or enjoy a glass of wine most every day, along with a dash of humor.

Cheers!
Tor

*Tor's chef jacket as founder of the Master Series on
Wine and Food at Beringer; signed by Julia Child,
Thomas Keller, Gary Danko, Joanne Weir, Cindy
Pawlcyn, and other chefs*

EPILOGUE:
BOTTLE SHOCKED

THIS BOOK WAS DONE. It was in the skilled and experienced hands of my editor and designer to make it pretty, accurate, and something we would be all proud of. My quiet year dodging COVID and fires had given birth to a child.

Destiny, circumstance, that unpredictable pinball that is my life, decided the book needed one more chapter. It was as if some Hollywood executive had read the script and looked around the table of "creatives" to say, "We need another ending."

I digress here with a story my father once told me. I never googled it, so I hope there is some accuracy in it. My father was a writer all his life. He had one great hit, a play called Cry *"Havoc,"* which went from a playhouse in Pasadena to Broadway to the silver screen in the 1940s before I was born. Nothing else matched this success in his career, but he wrote every day of his life. When he passed, I inherited his suitcases of unpublished material.

To keep food on our table, he did a lot of "script doctoring" for the movie studios and kept an ear to what was happening during writes and rewrites, Hollywood's favorite pastime. Faulkner, who spent a short stint in Hollywood, likened the process of turning a good book into a final script to taking a cow and turning it into a bouillon cube.

My father, while working on a certain cow for a certain studio, heard about a movie called *Shane*. Alan Ladd starred; it was a great story; it previewed and bombed. The studio hired the script doctors to fix it, and someone made a daring suggestion. The film was shot from Shane/Ladd's perspective—a hardened gunslinger trying to escape his past. Central to the story was a young boy who idolized Shane. Great movie. Great ending, which I'm not spoiling here. They reshot most of the movie again, this time from the boy's perspective, the camera looking up to Shane, and the movie became hugely successful—and deserved it.

So, I'm reshooting the ending here. My apologies off the bat. It allows me some freedom to clarify my perspective in critical areas dealing with the world of fine wine. Best of all, it tells a great story. It is the story of underdogs overcoming near impossible obstacles to find victory. I love the underdog and feel some affinity—I cried reading (and watching the adaptation of) Laura Hillenbrand's *Seabiscuit*. This chapter is about underdogs and perspective.

So, let's get to it.

JUDGMENT DAY NAPA VALLEY OCTOBER 6, 2021.
BOTTLE SHOCKED AGAIN—

OPENING SCENE The barrel room of the Charles Krug Winery, possibly the oldest continuously operating winery in the Napa Valley, founded in 1861. Several hundred invited guests have gathered to participate in a very special tasting and series of events leading up to it. Thirty-eight are "tasters," or in this case, judges. They range from famous wine writers and wine professionals (MW/master sommeliers)—seven in this grouping—to a larger group of thirty-one highly respected winemakers, wine writers/critics, and serious wine collectors who love fine wine and put their money where their heart is. If ever there was a representative group to judge wine, you could make an argument this was that group. Everyone was dead serious about what was expected from them.

They had to taste ten Chardonnays and ten Cabernet-based wines—*blind*. They had no idea who made the wines or where they were from. Their collective results would be heard and read around the world. Whether a movie would be made again, as in *Bottle Shock*, was a long shot. A very long shot, because the very first tasting was an accident, and this tasting had taken two years to stage. And this was not the first sequel to the original story.

FLASHBACKS 1976: In Paris, France, two expats, through a series of events, sit down in a room at the InterContinental hotel with a panel of nine highly respected French wine professionals. The expats, Steven Spurrier and Patricia Gallagher, had a handful of wines they had gathered (a story unto itself) of Napa Valley wines, and at the last minute, they decided to taste them against the French aristocracy of Bordeaux and Burgundy—wines that had pedigree. The Napa wines did not, and no one—*no one*—thought they would be taken seriously, even the organizers and the lone writer in the room from *Time* magazine, who also joined the party at the last minute to fill the time.

The original plan was to simply taste the California wines naked without a brown bag to hide their identity. But these underdogs did not have the respect of the French judges in the room, which was clear from the preliminary conversations. Aretha wanted R-E-S-P-E-C-T. Patricia and Steven wanted the same for the Americans. So at the last minute, all the wines were tasted blind. The judges were not thrilled but decided they could easily distinguish the French from the Californian wines, and it might be good fun after all.

The *Time* writer, George Taber, was enjoying the tasting and doodling until he realized the French experts were confusing the Bordeaux with the California Cabernets and the French Burgundies with the California Chardonnays. He began to take notes. Then the wines were identified. A Napa Valley Cabernet took first in its flight and the Napa Valley Chardonnay first in its flight, and the scores of other wines weighed California the winner of both tastings. The judges demanded their notes back. Too late—George had his story, filed it, and it appeared buried in the back pages of *Time* magazine. Just a few paragraphs, but they became legend.

In our very small wine world—it was the shot heard around the world. And the story has been told many times after growing an audience beyond our wine community: movies, books, documentaries, retastings. A few paragraphs became a whole library of opinion and retelling. There is a display of the winning wines in the Smithsonian.

Many critics of the results argued that it was a one-off, and the French wines with age would blow the California wines off the map. California wines just don't age, they claimed. So, twenty months later, another tasting was held in San Francisco at the Vintner Club, with Steven Spurrier flying out to officiate. The same set of California red wines cleaned house this time, placing first, second, third, and fourth.

In 1986, in New York at the French Culinary Institute (now the International Culinary Center) on the tenth anniversary, the same tasting with the same set of wines was held again. Different results, but California wines ranked one and two in the Cabernet tasting. The *Wine Spectator* held another tasting that year with four experts and two outsiders, and California Cabernets took the top five slots.

I was at the thirtieth anniversary tasting with the same set of wines (now getting very hard to find and increasingly expensive), which was held simultaneously in Napa Valley and at the historic Berry Bros. & Rudd cellar in London. The London judges included Michael Broadbent; Hugh Johnson; Jasper Morris, MW; and my friend Jancis Robinson, OBE, MW. The California Cabernets took the top five slots, the French Bordeaux the next four. I remember Steven Spurrier announcing their results from London over the loudspeaker. It was late there, and there seemed to be notes of conciliation, defeat, in his voice, but Steven also has a way of keeping things in perspective. It was all good fun. You beat us fair and square.

BACK TO KRUG, NAPA VALLEY—OCTOBER 6, 2021

At 10:30 A.M., the guests and judges enter the barrel room on the red carpet. Barrels surround the room, places for the thirty-eight judges in the middle, and big video screens and speakers in front. Guests found seats spaced around the room with full access to the screen and center stage.

Throughout the long process of staging this tasting during a pandemic, Steven Spurrier had died peacefully (of cancer), but not before event organizer Angela Duerr sent her crew to film hours of Steven talking about the original tasting in 1976—how it unfolded and its repercussions. Angela also had hours of George Taber on film talking about his role in the original and new tastings in Napa. His health made it impossible for him to travel, but he was all in and excited that the originators of the 1976 Paris Wine Tasting were all involved again—anticipating that another shot might be fired around the world, even if Steven would not hear it this time.

Patricia Gallagher, bless her, braved COVID travel restrictions and flew out from France to attend. She set the record straight in many respects: it was really her idea to hold the tasting and show off the California wines. Her excitement for the new tasting was palpable and very entertaining. I had lunch with her and Angela the next day and easily understood how important her determination was to the 1976 tasting.

After several hours of toasts and videos with other winemakers and wine industry leaders, we had a surprise appearance from Paul Draper, one of the industry's icons whose Ridge Vineyards Monte Bello Cabernet Sauvignon was in the original 1976 Tasting and its sequels. He read a letter from Bella Spurrier, thanking everyone on Steven's behalf for honoring him and the original tasting. It was moving; tears were shed.

I was included in several of the video clips taken over the months leading up to the tasting, including one in which I was asked what I thought might happen this time around. My answer was, anything could happen with a new set of judges and wines—but—*but*—my money was still on Napa. My tone was playful, maybe a bit tantalizing, which was my objective. In the end, we should not take the results too seriously. As Spurrier would have interjected, it was great fun to be front and center during an exciting horse race of champions.

So, who would be the new champs? Would the red wine champion still hail from Napa? Would there be outliers from new wine regions outside California and Bordeaux? There were so many story lines. Few knew the wines—maybe only Peter Marks, MW, who had chosen the wines, and his group of professional pourers.

Now, a disclaimer. I did know I had a horse in this race because I was asked to provide ten bottles for this tasting.

Finally, it was showtime, and the drumroll began. The wines were poured by a team of professional sommeliers from unmarked decanters. The judges were given thirty minutes to make their decisions, and I was immediately aware my heart had started to race. I tried to calm myself. I couldn't be an official judge because I had a wine in the tasting, but one of the judges let me taste her wines. Candidly, I did not immediately pick mine out—they were all great wines, or Peter would not have picked them. They were meant to represent the best Cabernet-based wines in the world. I tasted and kept my scores to myself. I grew calmer because finishing last would still be an honor. No disgrace to be in such company in this race.

Would a Seabiscuit wine, an underdog, running against a field with a more impressive pedigree, possibly win again? It had in the past.

The judges finally turned in their scores and were asked to talk about the wines. Curiously, most of their conversation was about whether they were from Napa Valley or Bordeaux, or someplace else. While Peter was tallying their rankings, Andy Beckstoffer appeared at my shoulder and asked me to bring him up to speed. I tried but must have been a little disjointed, for my heart was starting up again. I had not prepared for this.

Andrea Immer-Robinson, MS, had masterfully held the day together as emcee and was finally ready to announce the winners. She did so, but she was starting with the tenth-place wine and working slowly up to first. I secretly prayed I would place in the top five. Please, top five would be awesome.

They announced the bottom five, and I was not in that grouping. My heart was performing floor exercises against my rib cage. When Andrea

*Andy Beckstoffer and Tor first hearing the news
that their 2016 TOR Beckstoffer To Kalon won
the 2021 Judgment of Napa Tasting*

unveiled second place and my wine had not been announced, my jaw dropped to my navel, and I turned to Andy, speechless. Numb.

"OMG!" Andrea shouted out and unveiled our TOR Beckstoffer To Kalon as #1. Cannons went off; confetti rained down on the room. I stared at Andy, then we loaded up our arms and gave the audience one huge high five! I did a very poor impression of Tiger Woods holing a putt on 18 and was immediately surrounded by well-wishers.

Ladies and gentlemen, it was a great moment for me personally but more so for the entire team at the winery. Jeff Ames, the winemaker. He knows To Kalon; he knows each block of grapes we work with intimately. He shaped the wine that for that day in time was #1 and filled out the big screen in front of us. I combined both panels' scores later—the expert seven and the winemakers, writers, and collectors who made up the thirty-one others, and we still placed #1.

The Judgment of Napa, 2021, the moment the winning wine was announced

Hollywood ending. Seabiscuit beat War Admiral. The script doctors got their way.

Or did they?

I have talked to friends, writers, critics, and organizers, etc., and the reactions, or interpretations, of the Judgment of Napa are mixed. I also talked with a well-known Hollywood producer. Hollywood mogul Barry Baker had serendipitously arranged for a tasting with me a few days after the Judgment. He suggested getting Stanley Tucci to narrate then make a documentary with Angela's film rolls. Now *that* would be cool.

As with the original Paris Tasting of 1976, there are detractors. One argument is, it simply is a tasting or judgment of the wines at one point in time, with a group of judges who all have differing opinions. No two scorecards are alike. They are correct. It is not definitive. But it is fun.

Others found it an opportunity to get on their own soapbox, voicing their opinions about Napa Valley wines and French wines. With some, California will never get respect. We could do hundreds of tastings with French, Inuit, or Russian judges, and they would just not open their minds. That's okay. Over time, some points of view calcify then become fossils. It is hard breathing life into a fossil.

I was once tasting my wines with a collector who had been buying and enjoying wine for more than three decades, and he told me a story that bothered me for some time. Now I'm over it. He was at a restaurant in Northern California (south of San Francisco) that had a huge wine list, most of it old world, and much of it filled with wines many in the wine-drinking population would not be familiar with. I personally like these lists, but for many they are daunting.

Anyway, he asked the younger sommelier if he had any Napa Valley Cabernets on the list. He had a hard time finding them. The somm said a few but tried to guide him to Bordeaux or other old-world appellations. He explained he was interested in having a Napa Valley Cabernet that night. The somm hesitated, then announced, "Okay, but when you know more about wine, you will choose differently."

The man left the restaurant and has not returned.

Once again, it is usually someone who is six to ten years into being a wine professional, who purportedly knows everything. Before and after that narrow window, most of us are learning, broadening our frame of reference and opinions.

Dictating your point of view in wine is dangerous. It turns curious people off; it makes wine an elite beverage, and it is not. It is a wonderful beverage that should bring people together, not have them walk out of your restaurant.

More stories about the last Judgment Day continue to appear as time passes. Some have said the retelling of the Judgement of Paris has led to burnout. This was not evident at Krug on October 6. Patricia Gallagher told me at our long lunch the day after, she wants a Judgment Day every year, inviting the professional gambling world to take bets on the winners. I doubt this will happen. For me, like Steven and Patricia, I love a great horse race on a level and fair playing field. It is exciting, and it is good fun. It is also a huge amount of work and very expensive to execute. Not the simple accident that fostered the Judgment of Paris in 1976.

One local writer passed on the story because she felt stories about climate change, fires, earthquakes, and other disasters were more important. How can you argue against that? Can't. But I have realized, especially in the last year, I need a little entertainment in my life to lessen the blows of natural and unnatural disasters. I welcome a little playful diversion, a good story about underdogs carrying the day. These stories have become oxygen in a world that seems to be gasping for air. They are entertaining and give me hope. Winemakers survive on hope.

I have conducted thousands of wine tastings in my fortunate life, and I often hear the words from someone in the group that has gathered: "I'm not a connoisseur, so . . . , " and what follows is often self-deprecating or dismissive of their ability to know or appreciate good wine. I'm always bothered by this because it infers only an elite group can truly understand all the intricacies of fine wine. Wrong. Someone who tastes a well-made wine for the first time can have as much enjoyment and excitement as any wine professional. Maybe more. They might be analyzing it less and more focused on their sheer enjoyment. Wine is a world of stories about people who have struggled with failure and success, and in that alone, it can give pleasure. It is shaped by the human hand and nature.

So in passing, I invite you to be comfortable in the company of wine. Explore it if it invites you. If you like it a lot, you might find it takes you to new places and introduces you to new friends. You might have a lot of adventure on this journey. I did.

Cheers,
Tor
The end . . . for now.

CABERNET SAUVIGNON & BLENDS—
EVENT PANEL RESULTS

1. 2016 TOR Wines Cabernet Sauvignon, Beckstoffer To Kalon, Oakville, Napa Valley, California

2. 2016 Scarecrow Cabernet Sauvignon, Napa Valley, California

3. 2016 Château Léoville-Las Cases, St-Julien, 2ème Cru Classé, France

4. 2016 Colgin Cabernet Sauvignon, Tychson Hill, Napa Valley, California

5. 2016 Penfolds Cabernet Sauvignon, Bin 707, South Australia, Australia

6. 2016 Ornellaia, Bolgheri Superiore, Tuscany, Italy

7. 2016 Ridge Monte Bello, Santa Cruz Mountains, California

8. 2016 Château Mouton Rothschild, Pauillac, 1er Cru Classé, France

9. 2016 Château Montrose, St-Estèphe, 2ème Cru Classé, France

10. 2016 Viña Almaviva, Puente Alto, Maipo Valley, Chile

TOR

NAPA VALLEY
CABERNET SAUVIGNON

BECKSTOFFER
TO KALON VINEYARD

2016

Twenty-Five Barrels

ACKNOWLEDGMENTS

A special thanks to Maggy Walton: You kept my voice and made it clearer and stepped up whenever I needed you; you made it a fun journey, and for that I owe you a lot.

And to my agent, Leslie Stoker: You gave us a good home and a calendar. Thanks for your faith in me.

Thank you Chris, Iain, Jan, Suzi, and all my new friends at Cameron/Abrams. You made me look good, which I consider a bit of a miracle.

These are mentors and good friends I've shared wine and a table with over the years. In many ways, each inspired me to write this book. Thank you, all.

Susan, Molly, and Cooper
Mom and Dad
Rory, Kim, and Tandy Kenward
Maynard Amerine
Jeff Ames
Johnny Apple
Bart and Daphne Araujo
Gerald Asher
Andy and Betty Beckstoffer
Jimmy Cagney (thanks for those Vietnam
 letters of encouragement)
Pat Cetta
Julia Child
Roger Cleveland
Darrell Corti
Gary Danko
Jay and Kristine Eagan
Elvis—TCB
M. F. K. Fisher
Joe Heitz
Richard Helmstetter
Larry and Chris Hyde
Madeleine Kamman
Thomas Keller
Walt Klenz

James Laube
Bruce LeFavour and Faith Echtermeyer
Patrick Leon
Edna Lewis
Jean-Louis Mandrau
Karen MacNeil
Greg Melanson
Danny Meyer
Phil and Amy Mickelson
Robert and Margrit Mondavi
Mike Moone
Hal Oats
Robert Parker
Bruce and Heather Phillips
Colin Powell
Belle and Barney Rhodes
Nick and Jancis Robinson
Ed Sbragia
André Tchelistcheff
Jim Tonjum
Jeremiah Tower
Sandy and Joan Weill
Warren Winiarski
Kevin Zraly

Tor in his cellar